THE VISUAL
DICTIONARY *of*
CARS

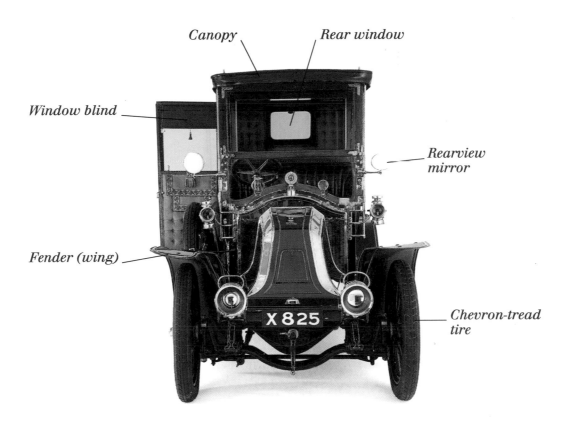

Canopy

Rear window

Window blind

Rearview mirror

Fender (wing)

X 825

Chevron-tread tire

FRONT VIEW OF 1906 RENAULT

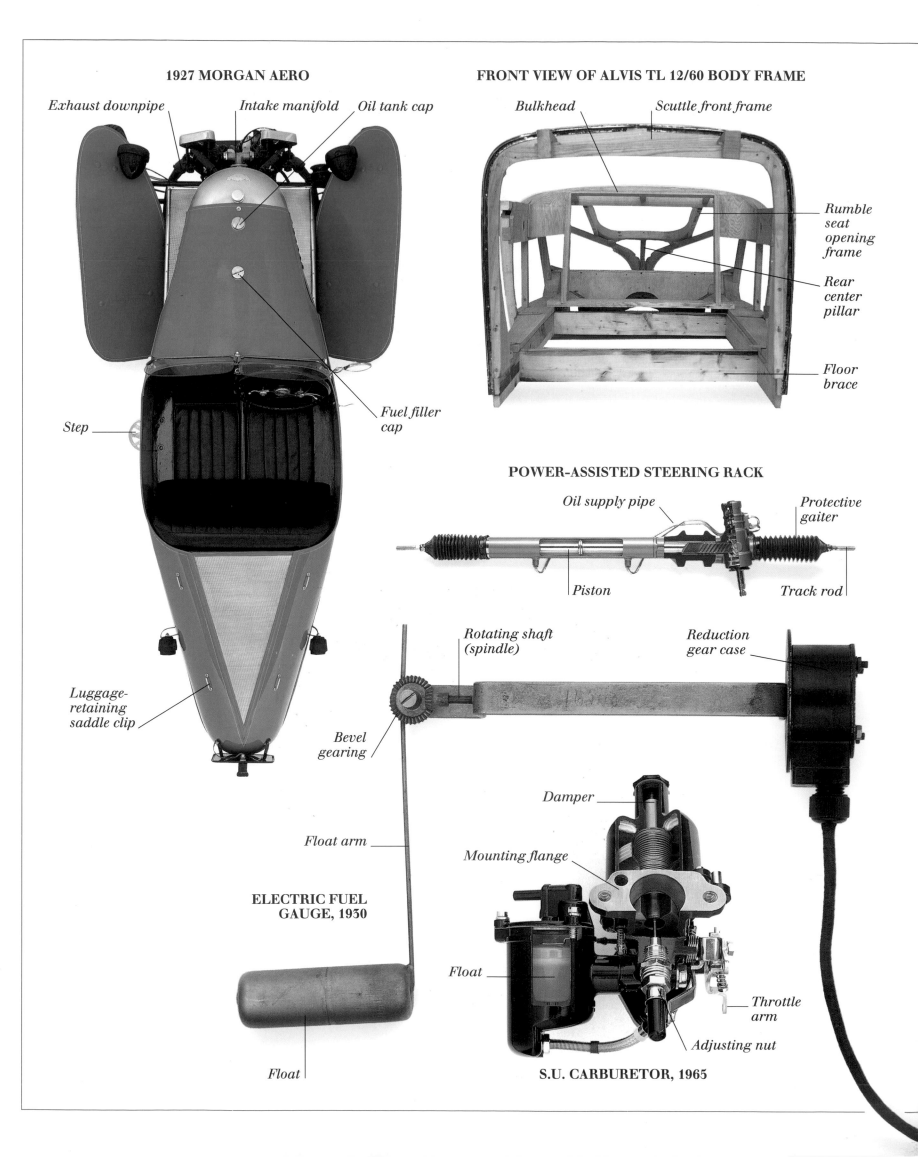

1927 MORGAN AERO

Exhaust downpipe

Intake manifold

Oil tank cap

Step

Fuel filler cap

Luggage-retaining saddle clip

ELECTRIC FUEL GAUGE, 1930

Float arm

Float

FRONT VIEW OF ALVIS TL 12/60 BODY FRAME

Bulkhead

Scuttle front frame

Rumble seat opening frame

Rear center pillar

Floor brace

POWER-ASSISTED STEERING RACK

Oil supply pipe

Protective gaiter

Piston

Track rod

Rotating shaft (spindle)

Reduction gear case

Bevel gearing

Damper

Mounting flange

Float

Throttle arm

Adjusting nut

S.U. CARBURETOR, 1965

EYEWITNESS VISUAL DICTIONARIES

THE VISUAL DICTIONARY *of* CARS

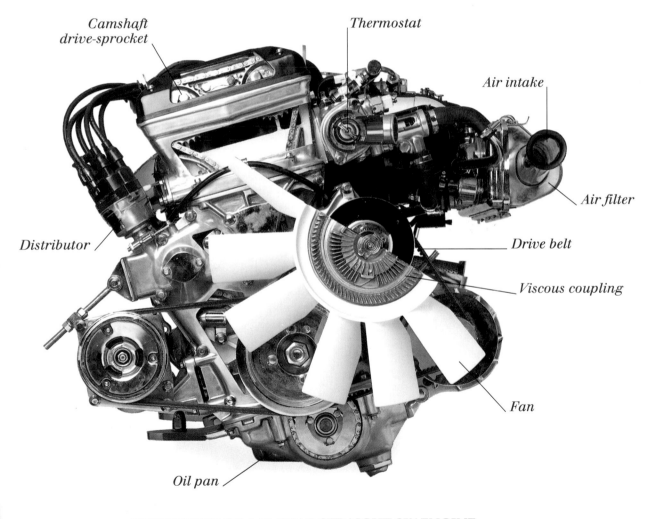

Camshaft drive-sprocket

Thermostat

Air intake

Air filter

Indicator needle

Distributor

Drive belt

Viscous coupling

PETROL

GALLONS

Fan

Oil pan

FRONT VIEW OF A JAGUAR STRAIGHT SIX ENGINE

Drive cable

DORLING KINDERSLEY, INC.

NEW YORK

A DORLING KINDERSLEY BOOK

Project Art Editor Nicola Liddiard
Designer Paul Calver

Project Editor Paul Docherty
Consultant Editor David Burgess-Wise
U.S. Consultant Jonathan A. Stein
U.S. Editor Charles Wills

Series Art Editor Stephen Knowlden
Series Editor Martyn Page
Art Director Chez Picthall
Managing Editor Ruth Midgley

Photography Simon Clay, John Lepine, Tim Ridley, Dave Rudkin
Illustrations Mick Gillah

Production Hilary Stephens

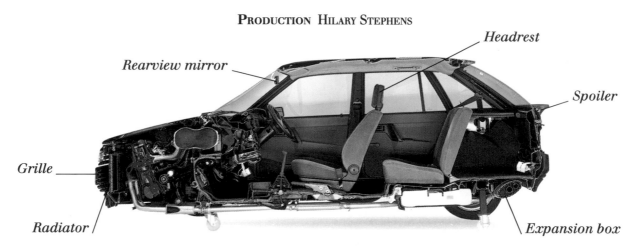

Rearview mirror

Headrest

Spoiler

Grille

Radiator

Expansion box

SECTIONED SEAT IBIZA

First American Edition, 1992

10 9 8 7 6 5 4 3 2 1

Dorling Kindersley, Inc., 232 Madison Avenue
New York, New York 10016

Library of Congress Cataloging-in-Publication Data

The Eyewitness visual dictionary of cars. — 1st American ed.
p. cm. — (The Eyewitness visual dictionaries)
Includes index.
Summary: Text and labeled illustrations depict a variety of
historical, classic, and contemporary automobiles and their components.
ISBN 1–56458–007–5 — ISBN 1–56458–008–3
1. Automobiles—Terminology—Juvenile literature.
2. Automobiles—Pictorial works—Juvenile literature.
3. Picture dictionaries, English—Juvenile literature.
[1. Automobiles.] I. Dorling Kindersley, Inc. II. Series.
TL206.E84 1992
629. 222'03—dc20   91–58205
                                      CIP
                                      AC

Reproduced by Colourscan, Singapore
Printed and bound by Arnoldo Mondadori, Verona, Italy

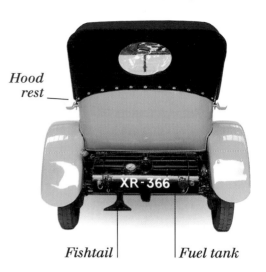

Folding
windshield

Honeycomb
radiator

Beam axle

**1913 ROLLS ROYCE SILVER
GHOST TOURER**

Hood
rest

Fishtail

Fuel tank

**1924 ROLLS ROYCE SILVER
GHOST TOURER**

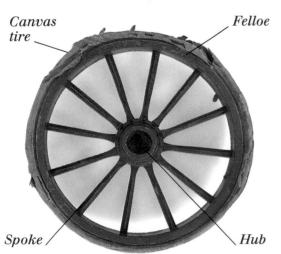

Gearbox

Fuel tank

**1932 15/18 HP LANCHESTER
RUNNING CHASSIS**

Canvas
tire

Felloe

Spoke

Hub

**ARTILLERY WHEEL
(WOODEN-SPOKED WHEEL)**

Contents

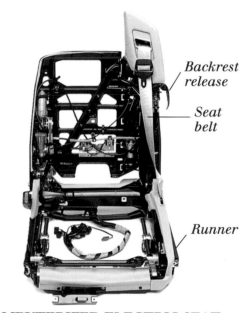

Backrest
release

Seat
belt

Runner

COMPUTERIZED ELECTRIC SEAT

Calorimeter

Radiator
cap

Radiator
badge

**ALFA ROMEO RADIATOR
AND GRILLE**

The first cars

THE EARLIEST ROAD VEHICLE powered by an engine, the Cugnot steam traction engine, was built in 1770. More practical steam carriages, such as the Bordino, were available in the early 19th century, but they were heavy and cumbersome. Restrictive laws and the introduction of railways, faster and able to carry more passengers, saw the decline of "cars" powered by steam. It was not until 1860 that the first practical power unit for road vehicles was developed with the invention of the internal combustion engine by the Belgian Étienne Lenoir. By around 1890, Karl Benz and Gottlieb Daimler in Germany and Albert de Dion and Armand Peugeot in France were building cars for sale to the public. These early cars, despite being primitive, expensive, and produced in limited numbers, heralded the age of the automobile.

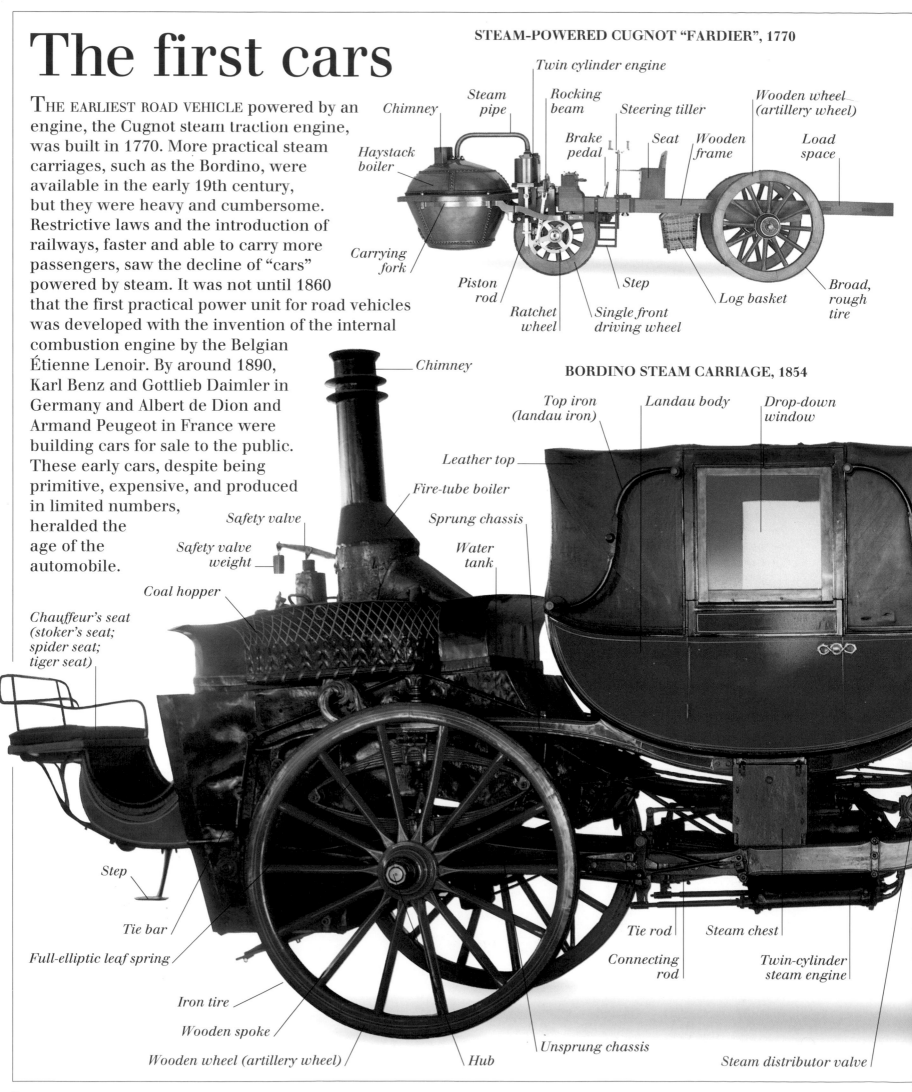

STEAM-POWERED CUGNOT "FARDIER", 1770

Twin cylinder engine
Chimney
Steam pipe
Rocking beam
Steering tiller
Wooden wheel (artillery wheel)
Brake pedal
Seat
Wooden frame
Load space
Haystack boiler
Carrying fork
Piston rod
Step
Log basket
Broad, rough tire
Ratchet wheel
Single front driving wheel

BORDINO STEAM CARRIAGE, 1854

Chimney
Top iron (landau iron)
Landau body
Drop-down window
Leather top
Fire-tube boiler
Sprung chassis
Safety valve
Safety valve weight
Water tank
Coal hopper
Chauffeur's seat (stoker's seat; spider seat; tiger seat)
Step
Tie bar
Full-elliptic leaf spring
Iron tire
Wooden spoke
Wooden wheel (artillery wheel)
Hub
Unsprung chassis
Tie rod
Steam chest
Connecting rod
Twin-cylinder steam engine
Steam distributor valve

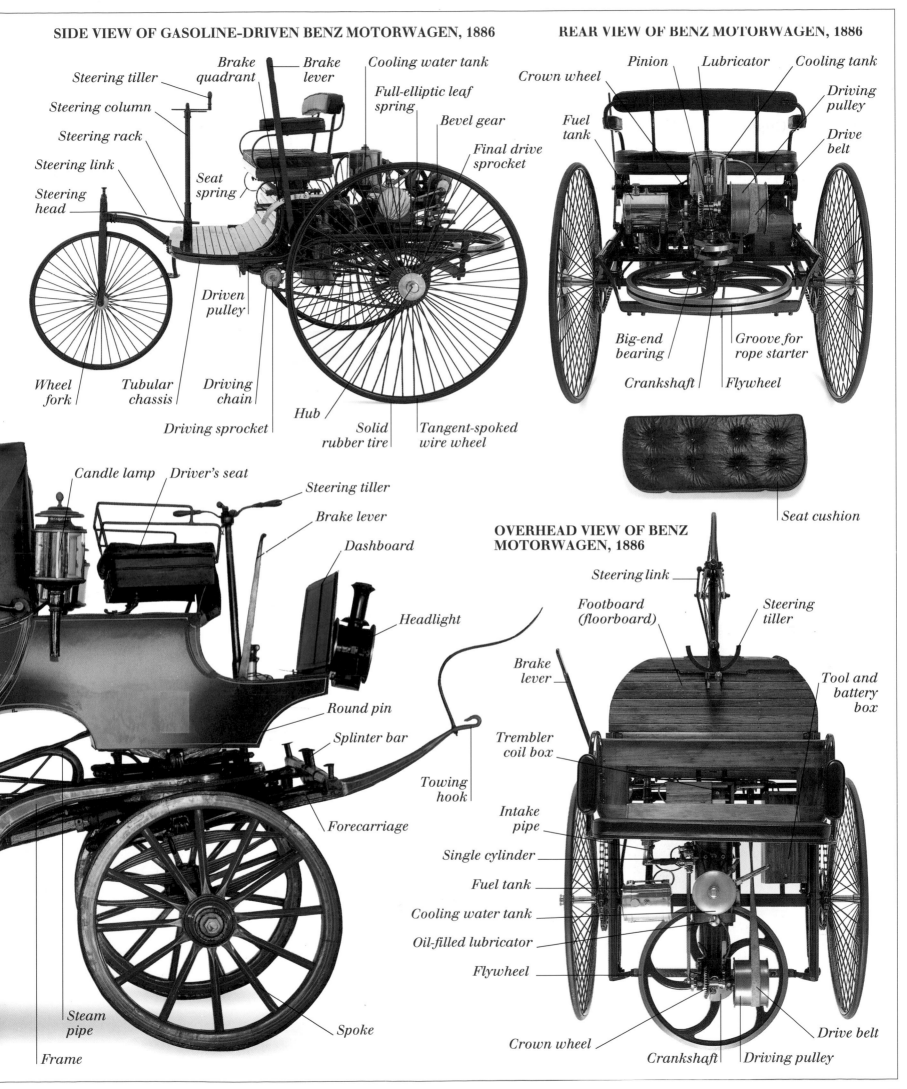

SIDE VIEW OF GASOLINE-DRIVEN BENZ MOTORWAGEN, 1886

Steering tiller

Steering column

Steering rack

Steering link

Steering head

Brake quadrant

Brake lever

Cooling water tank

Full-elliptic leaf spring

Bevel gear

Final drive sprocket

Seat spring

Driven pulley

Wheel fork

Tubular chassis

Driving chain

Driving sprocket

Hub

Solid rubber tire

Tangent-spoked wire wheel

REAR VIEW OF BENZ MOTORWAGEN, 1886

Crown wheel

Pinion

Lubricator

Cooling tank

Driving pulley

Drive belt

Fuel tank

Big-end bearing

Groove for rope starter

Crankshaft

Flywheel

Seat cushion

Candle lamp

Driver's seat

Steering tiller

Brake lever

Dashboard

Headlight

Round pin

Splinter bar

Towing hook

Forecarriage

Steam pipe

Spoke

Frame

OVERHEAD VIEW OF BENZ MOTORWAGEN, 1886

Steering link

Footboard (floorboard)

Steering tiller

Tool and battery box

Brake lever

Trembler coil box

Intake pipe

Single cylinder

Fuel tank

Cooling water tank

Oil-filled lubricator

Flywheel

Crown wheel

Crankshaft

Driving pulley

Drive belt

7

Elegance and utility

DURING THE FIRST DECADE OF THIS CENTURY, the motorist who could afford it had a choice of some of the finest cars ever made. These handbuilt cars were powerful and luxurious, using the finest wood, leather, and cloth, and bodywork made to the customer's individual requirements. Some had six-cylinder engines as big as 15 liters. The price of such cars was several times that of an average house, and their yearly running costs were also very high. As a result, basic, utilitarian cars became popular. Costing perhaps one-tenth of the price of a luxury car, these cars had very little trim and often had only single-cylinder engines.

1904 OLDSMOBILE SINGLE-CYLINDER ENGINE

Oil bottle dripfeed
Crankcase
Starting handle bracket
Exhaust pipe
Cylinder head
Cylinder
Starter cog
Carburetor
Engine timing gear
Crankshaft
Flywheel
Gear band

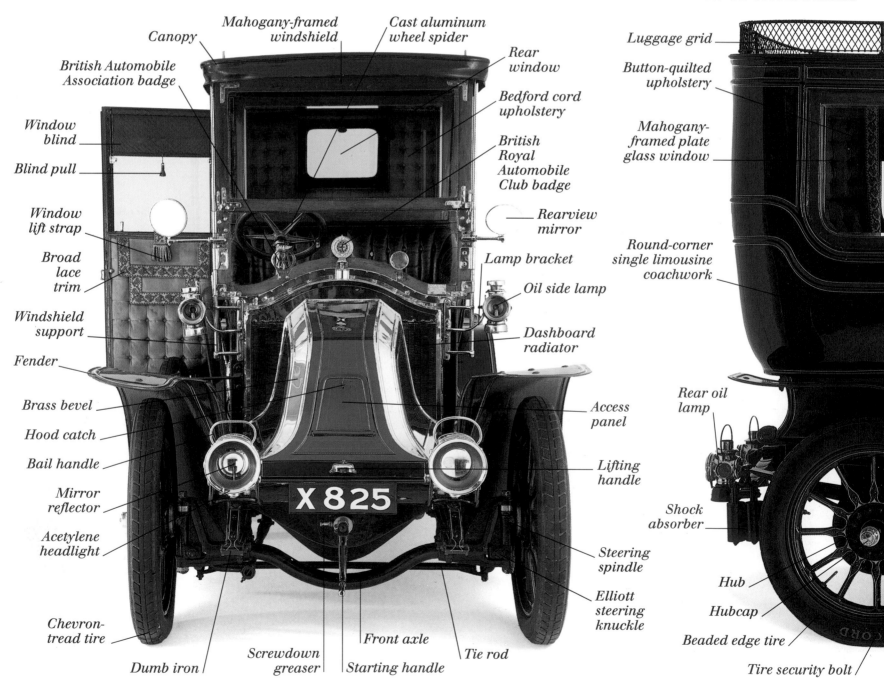

FRONT VIEW OF 1906 RENAULT

Canopy
Mahogany-framed windshield
Cast aluminum wheel spider
Rear window
British Automobile Association badge
Bedford cord upholstery
British Royal Automobile Club badge
Window blind
Blind pull
Window lift strap
Rearview mirror
Broad lace trim
Lamp bracket
Oil side lamp
Windshield support
Dashboard radiator
Fender
Brass bevel
Hood catch
Bail handle
Access panel
Mirror reflector
Lifting handle
Acetylene headlight
Steering spindle
Elliott steering knuckle
Chevron-tread tire
Dumb iron
Screwdown greaser
Front axle
Starting handle
Tie rod

SIDE VIEW OF 1906 RENAULT

Luggage grid
Button-quilted upholstery
Mahogany-framed plate glass window
Round-corner single limousine coachwork
Rear oil lamp
Shock absorber
Hub
Hubcap
Beaded edge tire
Tire security bolt

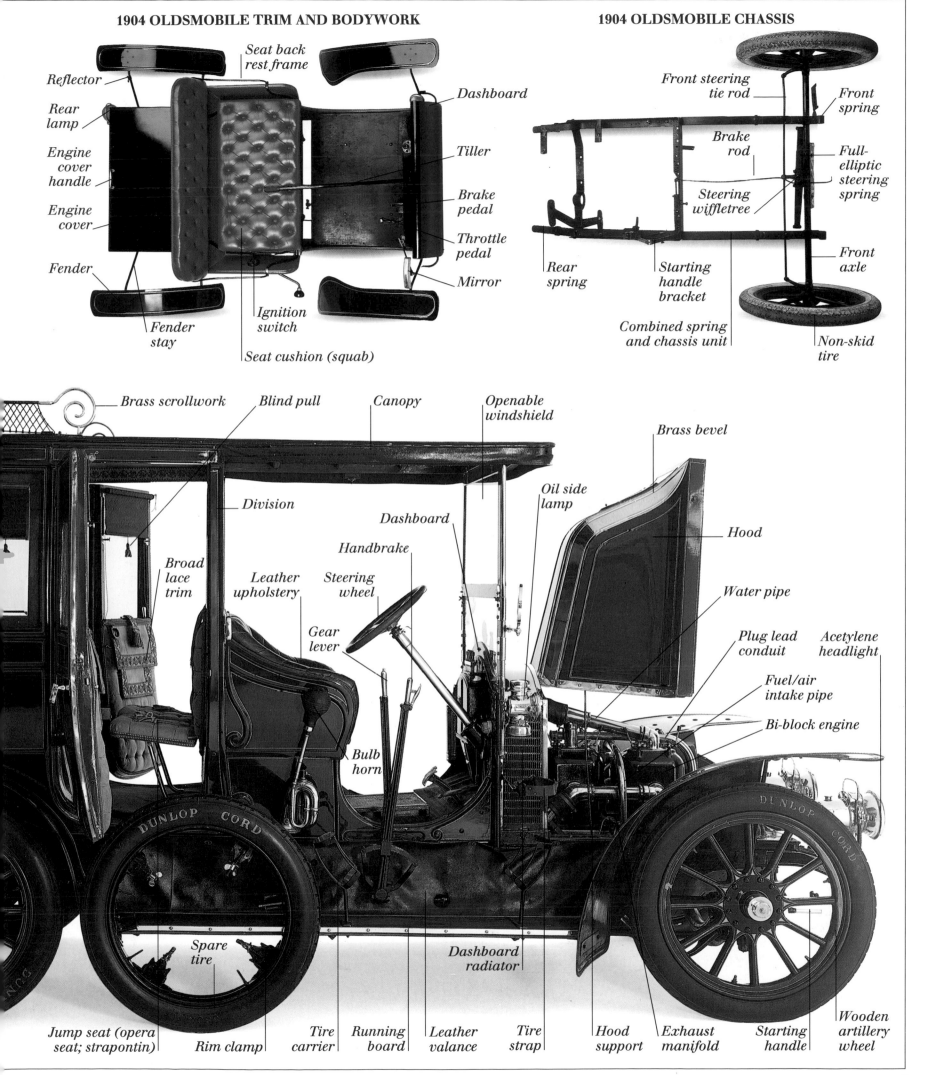

1904 OLDSMOBILE TRIM AND BODYWORK

- Reflector
- Rear lamp
- Engine cover handle
- Engine cover
- Fender
- Fender stay
- Ignition switch
- Seat cushion (squab)
- Seat back rest frame
- Dashboard
- Tiller
- Brake pedal
- Throttle pedal
- Mirror

1904 OLDSMOBILE CHASSIS

- Front steering tie rod
- Front spring
- Brake rod
- Full-elliptic steering spring
- Steering wiffletree
- Rear spring
- Starting handle bracket
- Front axle
- Combined spring and chassis unit
- Non-skid tire

- Brass scrollwork
- Blind pull
- Canopy
- Openable windshield
- Brass bevel
- Oil side lamp
- Hood
- Division
- Dashboard
- Water pipe
- Broad lace trim
- Leather upholstery
- Handbrake
- Steering wheel
- Plug lead conduit
- Acetylene headlight
- Gear lever
- Fuel/air intake pipe
- Bi-block engine
- Bulb horn
- Spare tire
- Dashboard radiator
- Jump seat (opera seat; strapontin)
- Rim clamp
- Tire carrier
- Running board
- Leather valance
- Tire strap
- Hood support
- Exhaust manifold
- Starting handle
- Wooden artillery wheel

Mass production

THE FIRST CARS WERE HAND-ASSEMBLED from individually built parts, a time-consuming procedure that required skilled mechanics and made cars very expensive. This problem was solved, in America, by a Detroit car manufacturer named Henry Ford. He introduced mass production by using standardized parts, and later combined these with a moving production line. The work was brought to the workers, each of whom performed one simple task in the construction process as the chassis moved along the line. The first mass-produced car, the Ford Model T, was launched in 1908. At first it was available in a limited range of body styles and colors. However, when the production line was introduced in 1914, the color range was cut back; the Model T became available, as Henry Ford said, in "any color you like, so long as it's black." Ford cut the production time for a car from several days to about 12 hours, and eventually to minutes, making cars much cheaper than before. As a result, half the cars in the world were Model T Fords by 1920.

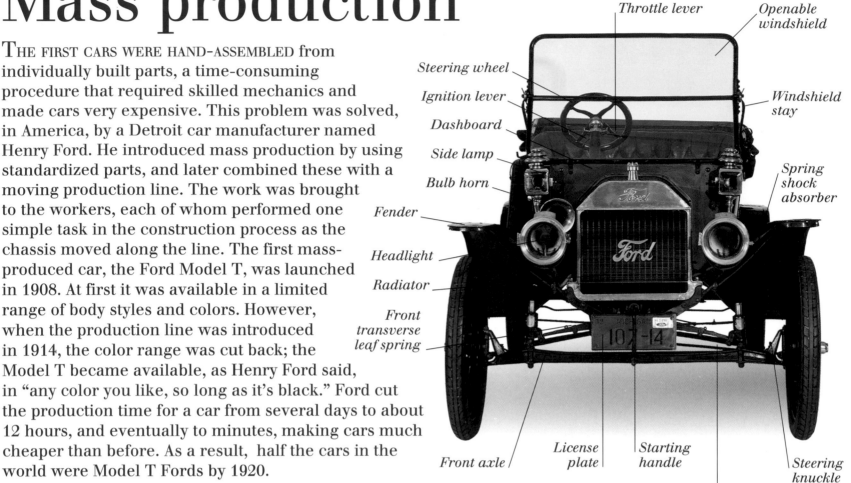

STAGES OF FORD MODEL T PRODUCTION

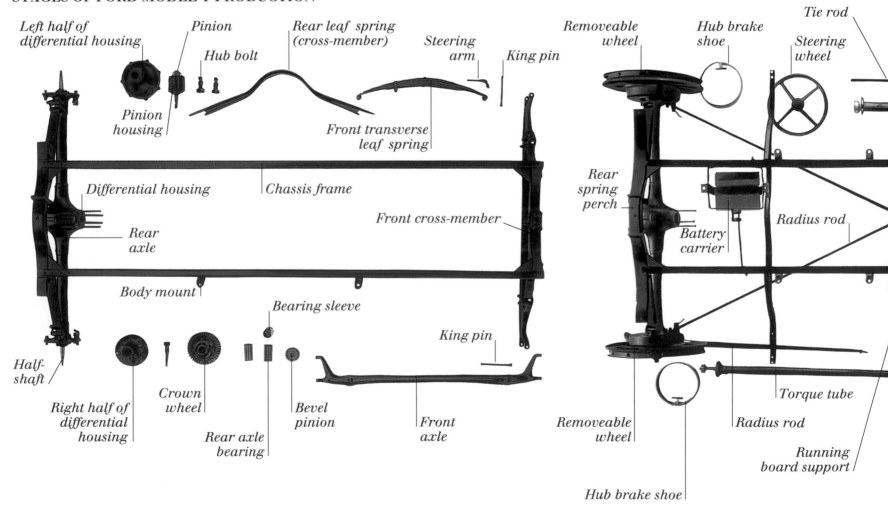

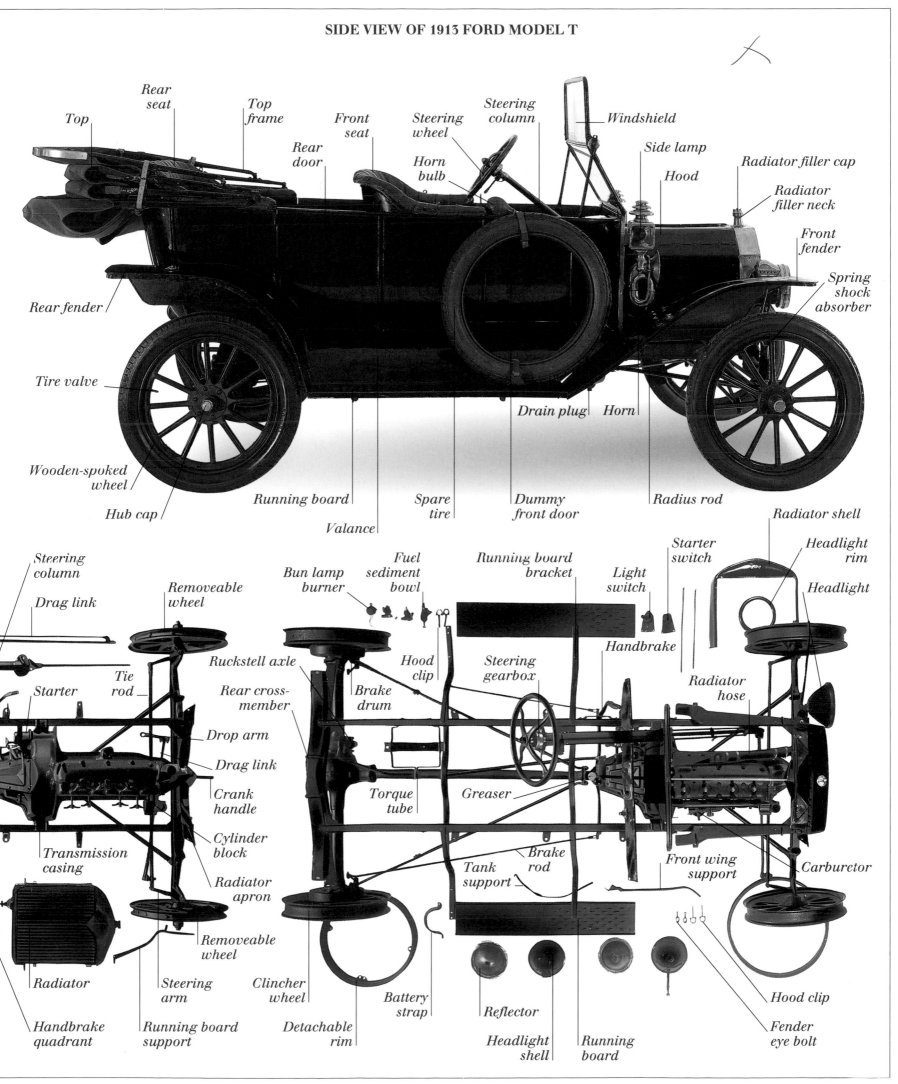

Top

Rear seat

Top frame

Front seat

Rear door

Steering wheel

Steering column

Horn bulb

Windshield

Side lamp

Hood

Radiator filler cap

Radiator filler neck

Front fender

Spring shock absorber

Rear fender

Tire valve

Drain plug

Horn

Wooden-spoked wheel

Hub cap

Valance

Running board

Spare tire

Dummy front door

Radius rod

Steering column

Drag link

Removeable wheel

Bun lamp burner

Fuel sediment bowl

Running board bracket

Light switch

Starter switch

Radiator shell

Headlight rim

Headlight

Starter

Tie rod

Ruckstell axle

Hood clip

Steering gearbox

Handbrake

Radiator hose

Rear cross-member

Brake drum

Drop arm

Drag link

Torque tube

Greaser

Crank handle

Transmission casing

Cylinder block

Brake rod

Front wing support

Carburetor

Radiator apron

Tank support

Removeable wheel

Radiator

Steering arm

Clincher wheel

Battery strap

Reflector

Hood clip

Handbrake quadrant

Running board support

Detachable rim

Headlight shell

Running board

Fender eye bolt

The "people's car"

THE MOST POPULAR CAR in the history of car manufacture is the Volkswagen Beetle, originally called the KdF Wagen. The car was developed in Germany in the 1930s by Dr. Ferdinand Porsche. At that time, Germany had only half the number of cars of Britain or France, and Adolf Hitler took a personal interest in the development of the Volkswagen ("people's car"). The intention was to provide a new industry, new jobs, and a car so inexpensive that anyone with a job could afford it. Dr. Porsche designed a car that was cheap to build and run; its rear-mounted, air-cooled engine cut down the number of parts needed and also reduced weight. However, few civilians managed to obtain the Beetle before the outbreak of the Second World War in 1939. After the war, the Beetle proved so popular that eventually more than 20 million were sold.

CUSTOMIZED VOLKSWAGEN BEETLE

FLAT-FOUR CYLINDER ARRANGEMENT

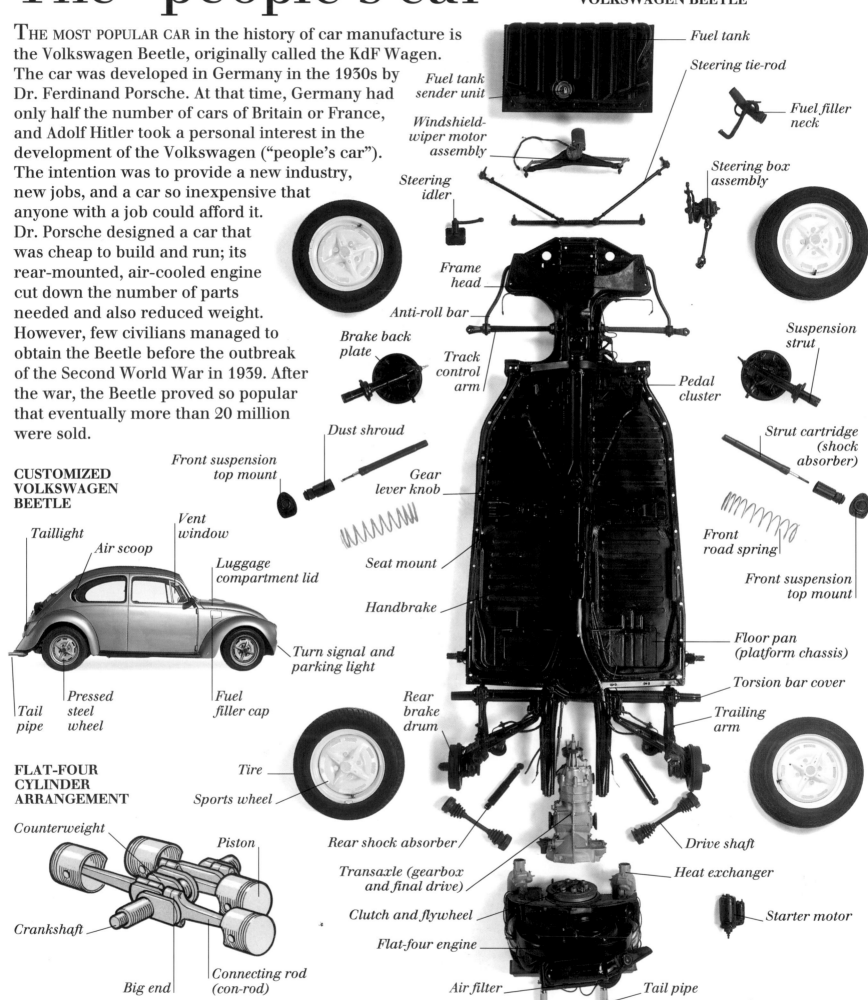

Fuel tank
Fuel tank sender unit
Steering tie-rod
Fuel filler neck
Windshield-wiper motor assembly
Steering box assembly
Steering idler
Frame head
Anti-roll bar
Suspension strut
Brake back plate
Track control arm
Pedal cluster
Dust shroud
Strut cartridge (shock absorber)
Front suspension top mount
Gear lever knob
Seat mount
Front road spring
Handbrake
Front suspension top mount
Floor pan (platform chassis)
Torsion bar cover
Rear brake drum
Trailing arm
Taillight
Air scoop
Vent window
Luggage compartment lid
Turn signal and parking light
Tail pipe
Pressed steel wheel
Fuel filler cap
Tire
Sports wheel
Rear shock absorber
Drive shaft
Transaxle (gearbox and final drive)
Heat exchanger
Counterweight
Piston
Clutch and flywheel
Starter motor
Crankshaft
Flat-four engine
Big end
Connecting rod (con-rod)
Air filter
Tail pipe

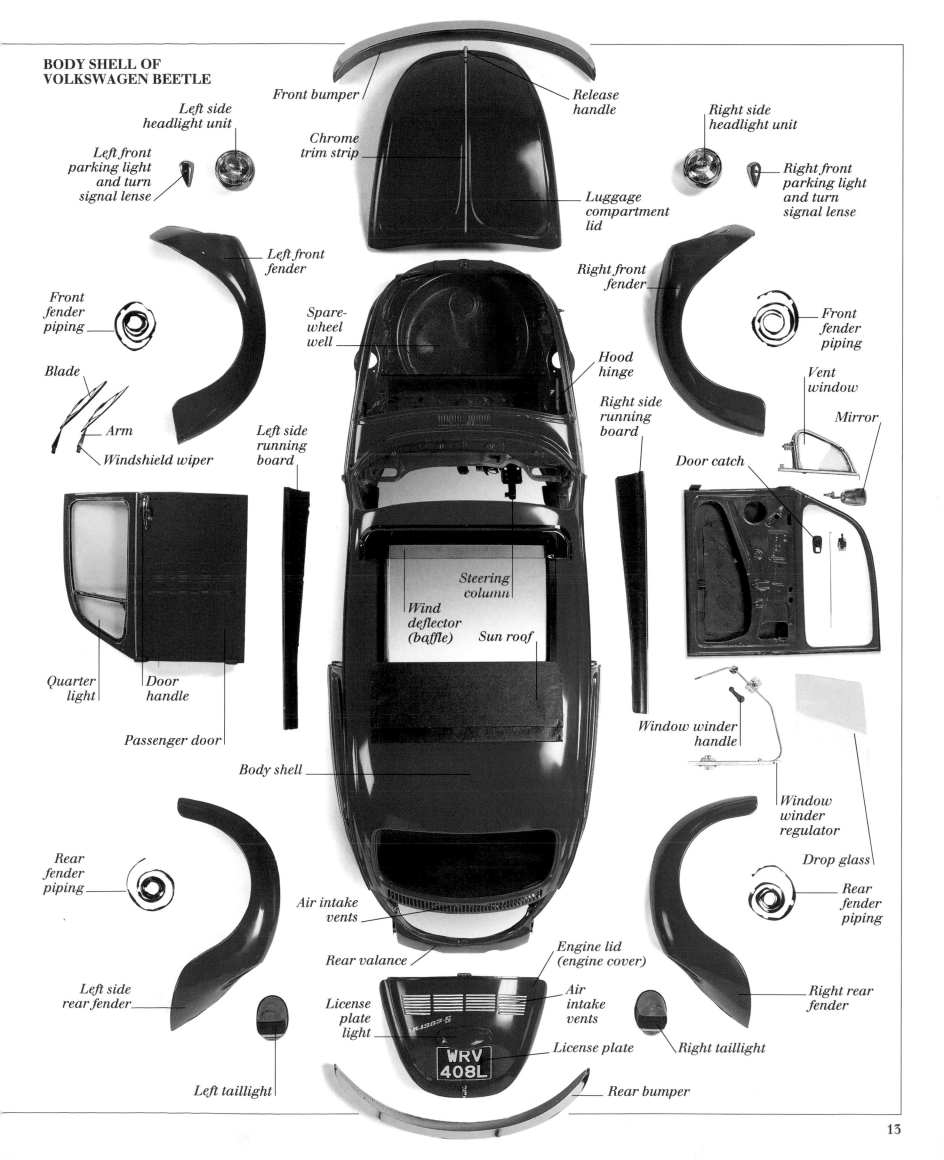

BODY SHELL OF VOLKSWAGEN BEETLE

Front bumper

Release handle

Left side headlight unit

Right side headlight unit

Chrome trim strip

Left front parking light and turn signal lense

Right front parking light and turn signal lense

Luggage compartment lid

Left front fender

Right front fender

Front fender piping

Spare-wheel well

Hood hinge

Front fender piping

Blade

Vent window

Mirror

Right side running board

Arm

Left side running board

Door catch

Windshield wiper

Steering column

Wind deflector (baffle)

Sun roof

Quarter light

Door handle

Window winder handle

Passenger door

Body shell

Window winder regulator

Drop glass

Rear fender piping

Rear fender piping

Air intake vents

Engine lid (engine cover)

Rear valance

Air intake vents

Left side rear fender

License plate light

Right rear fender

License plate

Right taillight

Left taillight

WRV 408L

Rear bumper

13

Early engines

STEAM AND ELECTRICITY were used to power cars until early this century, but neither power source was ideal. Electric cars had to stop frequently to recharge their heavy batteries, and steam cars gave smooth power delivery but were too complicated for the average motorist to use. A rival power source, the internal combustion engine, was invented in 1860 by Étienne Lenoir (see pp. 6-7). This engine converted the force of an explosion into rotary motion to turn the wheels of a vehicle. Early variations on this basic model included sleeve valves, separately cast cylinders, and the two-stroke combustion cycle. Today, all combustion engines, including the Wankel rotary and diesels (see pp. 18-19), use the four-stroke cycle, first demonstrated by Nikolaus Otto in 1876. The Otto cycle has proved the best method of ensuring that the engine turns over smoothly and that exhaust emissions are controllable.

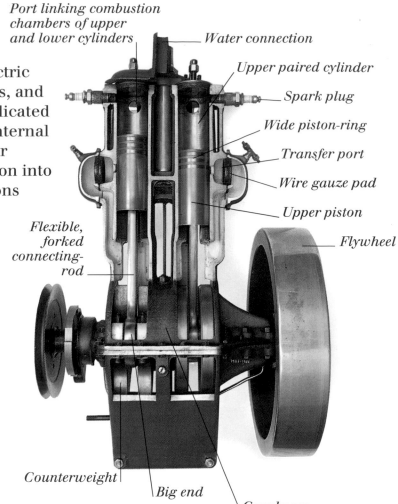

TROJAN TWO-STROKE ENGINE, 1927

Port linking combustion chambers of upper and lower cylinders

Water connection

Upper paired cylinder

Spark plug

Wide piston-ring

Transfer port

Wire gauze pad

Upper piston

Flexible, forked connecting-rod

Flywheel

Counterweight

Big end

Crankcase

BERSEY ELECTRIC CAB, 1896

Mounting for tray of 40 batteries

Housing for electric motors

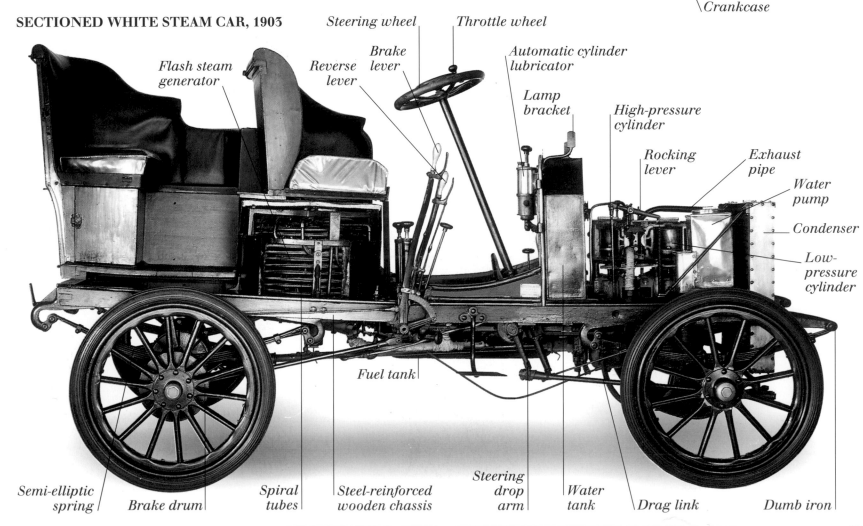

SECTIONED WHITE STEAM CAR, 1903

Steering wheel

Throttle wheel

Brake lever

Reverse lever

Flash steam generator

Automatic cylinder lubricator

Lamp bracket

High-pressure cylinder

Rocking lever

Exhaust pipe

Water pump

Condenser

Low-pressure cylinder

Fuel tank

Semi-elliptic spring

Brake drum

Spiral tubes

Steel-reinforced wooden chassis

Steering drop arm

Water tank

Drag link

Dumb iron

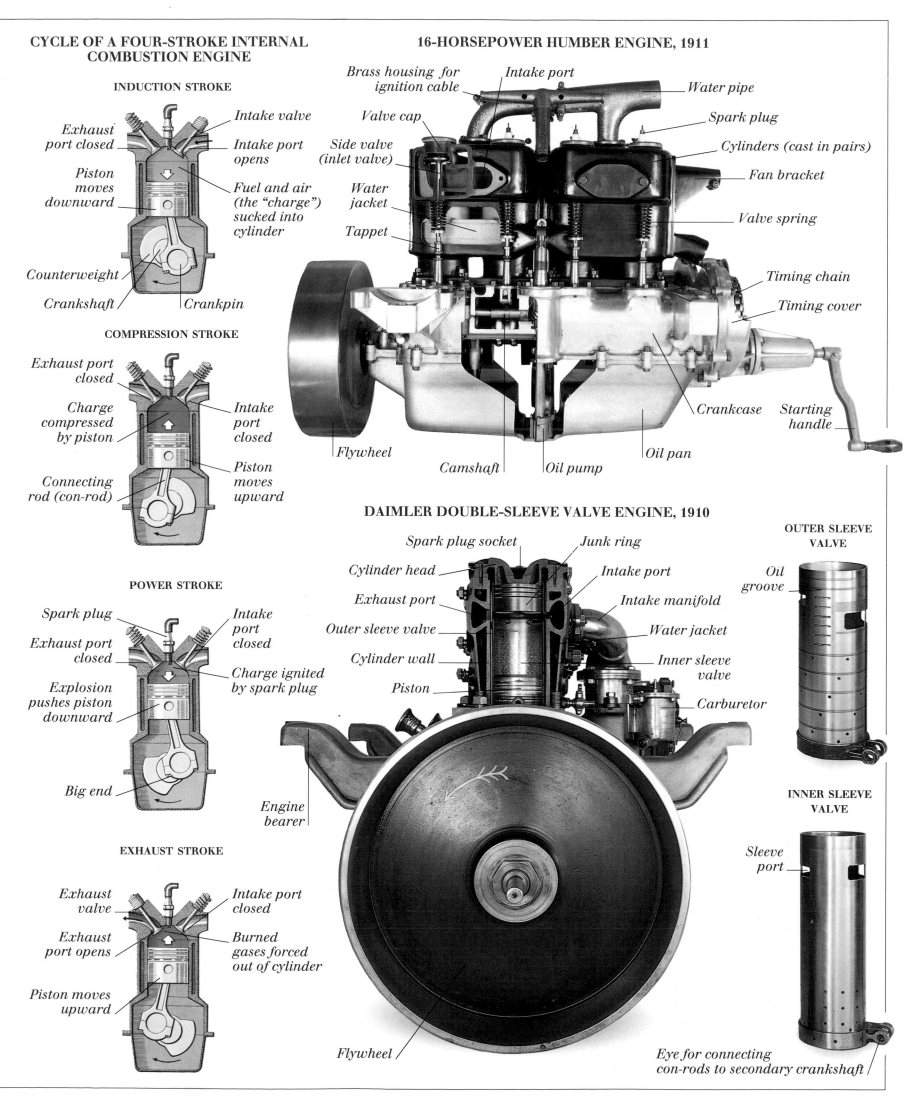

CYCLE OF A FOUR-STROKE INTERNAL COMBUSTION ENGINE

INDUCTION STROKE

Exhaust port closed
Intake valve
Intake port opens
Piston moves downward
Fuel and air (the "charge") sucked into cylinder
Counterweight
Crankshaft
Crankpin

COMPRESSION STROKE

Exhaust port closed
Charge compressed by piston
Intake port closed
Connecting rod (con-rod)
Piston moves upward

POWER STROKE

Spark plug
Intake port closed
Exhaust port closed
Charge ignited by spark plug
Explosion pushes piston downward
Big end

EXHAUST STROKE

Exhaust valve
Intake port closed
Exhaust port opens
Burned gases forced out of cylinder
Piston moves upward

16-HORSEPOWER HUMBER ENGINE, 1911

Brass housing for ignition cable
Intake port
Water pipe
Valve cap
Spark plug
Side valve (inlet valve)
Cylinders (cast in pairs)
Water jacket
Fan bracket
Tappet
Valve spring
Timing chain
Timing cover
Crankcase
Starting handle
Flywheel
Camshaft
Oil pump
Oil pan

DAIMLER DOUBLE-SLEEVE VALVE ENGINE, 1910

Spark plug socket
Junk ring
Cylinder head
Intake port
Exhaust port
Intake manifold
Outer sleeve valve
Water jacket
Cylinder wall
Inner sleeve valve
Piston
Carburetor
Engine bearer
Flywheel

OUTER SLEEVE VALVE

Oil groove

INNER SLEEVE VALVE

Sleeve port
Eye for connecting con-rods to secondary crankshaft

15

Modern engines

TODAY'S GASOLINE ENGINE WORKS on the same basic principles as the first car engines of a century ago, although it has been greatly refined. Modern engines, often made from special metal alloys, are much lighter than earlier engines. Computerized ignition systems (see pp. 22-23), fuel injectors (see pp. 24-25), and multi-valve cylinder heads achieve a more efficient combustion of the fuel/air mixture (the charge) so that less fuel is wasted. As a result of this greater efficiency, the power and performance of a modern engine are increased, and the level of pollution in the exhaust gases is reduced. Exhaust pollution levels today are also lowered by the increasing use of special filters called catalytic converters which absorb many exhaust pollutants. The need to produce ever more efficient engines means that it can take up to seven years to develop a new engine for a family car, at a cost of many millions of dollars.

FRONT VIEW OF A FORD COSWORTH V6 12-VALVE

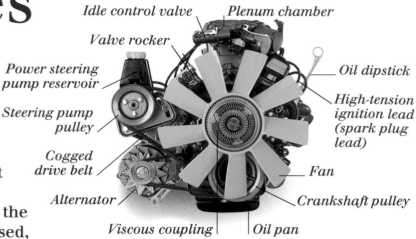

Idle control valve
Plenum chamber
Valve rocker
Power steering pump reservoir
Steering pump pulley
Cogged drive belt
Alternator
Viscous coupling
Oil pan
Oil dipstick
High-tension ignition lead (spark plug lead)
Fan
Crankshaft pulley

FRONT VIEW OF A FORD COSWORTH V6 24-VALVE

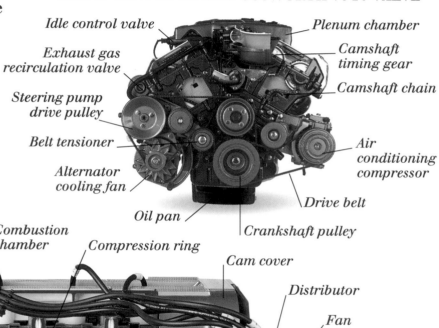

Idle control valve
Exhaust gas recirculation valve
Steering pump drive pulley
Belt tensioner
Alternator cooling fan
Oil pan
Plenum chamber
Camshaft timing gear
Camshaft chain
Air conditioning compressor
Drive belt
Crankshaft pulley

SECTIONED VIEW OF A JAGUAR STRAIGHT 6

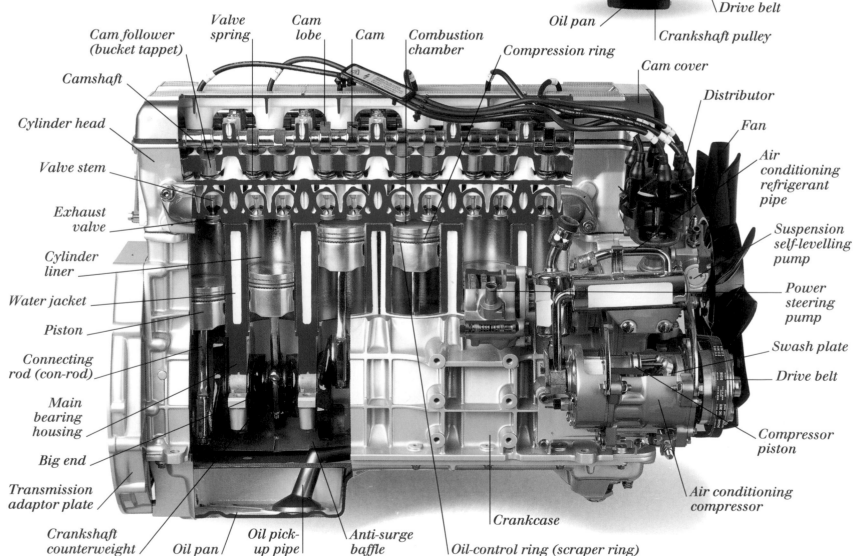

Valve spring
Cam lobe
Cam
Combustion chamber
Compression ring
Cam follower (bucket tappet)
Camshaft
Cylinder head
Valve stem
Exhaust valve
Cylinder liner
Water jacket
Piston
Connecting rod (con-rod)
Main bearing housing
Big end
Transmission adaptor plate
Crankshaft counterweight
Oil pan
Oil pick-up pipe
Anti-surge baffle
Crankcase
Oil-control ring (scraper ring)
Air conditioning compressor
Compressor piston
Drive belt
Swash plate
Power steering pump
Suspension self-levelling pump
Air conditioning refrigerant pipe
Fan
Distributor
Cam cover

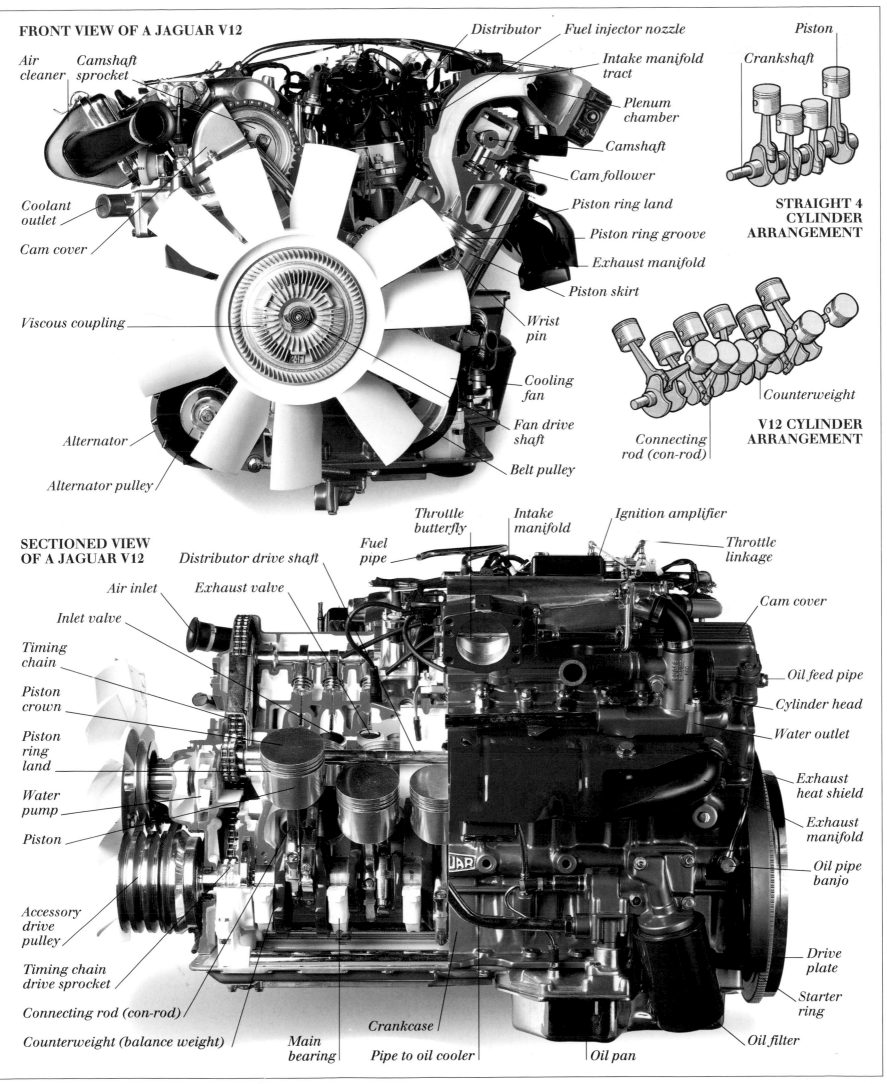

FRONT VIEW OF A JAGUAR V12

Distributor

Fuel injector nozzle

Piston

Air cleaner

Camshaft sprocket

Intake manifold tract

Crankshaft

Plenum chamber

Camshaft

STRAIGHT 4 CYLINDER ARRANGEMENT

Cam follower

Coolant outlet

Piston ring land

Cam cover

Piston ring groove

Exhaust manifold

Piston skirt

Viscous coupling

Wrist pin

Cooling fan

Counterweight

Fan drive shaft

V12 CYLINDER ARRANGEMENT

Alternator

Connecting rod (con-rod)

Alternator pulley

Belt pulley

SECTIONED VIEW OF A JAGUAR V12

Throttle butterfly

Intake manifold

Ignition amplifier

Throttle linkage

Fuel pipe

Distributor drive shaft

Air inlet

Exhaust valve

Cam cover

Inlet valve

Oil feed pipe

Timing chain

Cylinder head

Piston crown

Water outlet

Piston ring land

Exhaust heat shield

Water pump

Exhaust manifold

Piston

Oil pipe banjo

Accessory drive pulley

Drive plate

Timing chain drive sprocket

Starter ring

Connecting rod (con-rod)

Counterweight (balance weight)

Main bearing

Crankcase

Pipe to oil cooler

Oil pan

Oil filter

17

Alternative engines

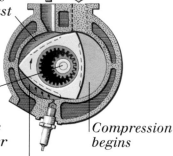

THE MOST COMMON TYPE OF ALTERNATIVE ENGINE is the diesel engine. Instead of igniting the compressed fuel/air mixture with a spark, the diesel engine uses compression alone, which heats the mixture to the point where it explodes. A diesel engine's fuel consumption is low in comparison with similarly sized piston engines, despite its heavier, reinforced moving parts and cylinder block. Another type of engine is the rotary-combustion, first successfully developed by Felix Wankel in the 1950s. Its two trilobate (three-sided) rotors revolve in housings shaped in a fat figure eight. The four sequences of the four-stroke cycle, which occur consecutively in a piston engine, occur simultaneously in a rotary engine, producing power in a continuous stream.

Aerodynamic windshield

Headrest

Top boot

Front spoiler (chin spoiler)

Side marker lamp

Body-side molding

Cast alloy wheel

WANKEL ROTARY ENGINE

OIL-PUMP HOUSING

FRONT SIDE HOUSING

FRONT ROTOR CHAMBER

INTERMEDIATE HOUSING

REAR ROTOR CHAMBER

Intake port

Trailing spark plug hole

Dipstick tube

Oil filler

Intake port

Aluminum alloy backing

Distributor fixing point (drive point)

Oil-pump drive

Coolant passage

Leading spark plug hole

Exhaust port

Water drain bolt

Trailing spark plug hole

Leading spark plug hole

THE WANKEL ROTARY CYCLE

Exhaust port

Intake port

Fuel/air mixture being compressed

Water passage

Burning gas expands

Trilobate rotor

Gas continues to expand

Exhaust port closed

Vacuum sucks in fuel/air mixture

Stationary gear (fixed gear)

Compression continues

Burnt gas exhausts

Rotor gear

Compressed gas ignites

Output shaft turns

Burnt gas continues to exhaust

Fuel/air mixture continues to enter

Burnt gas begins to expand

Compression begins

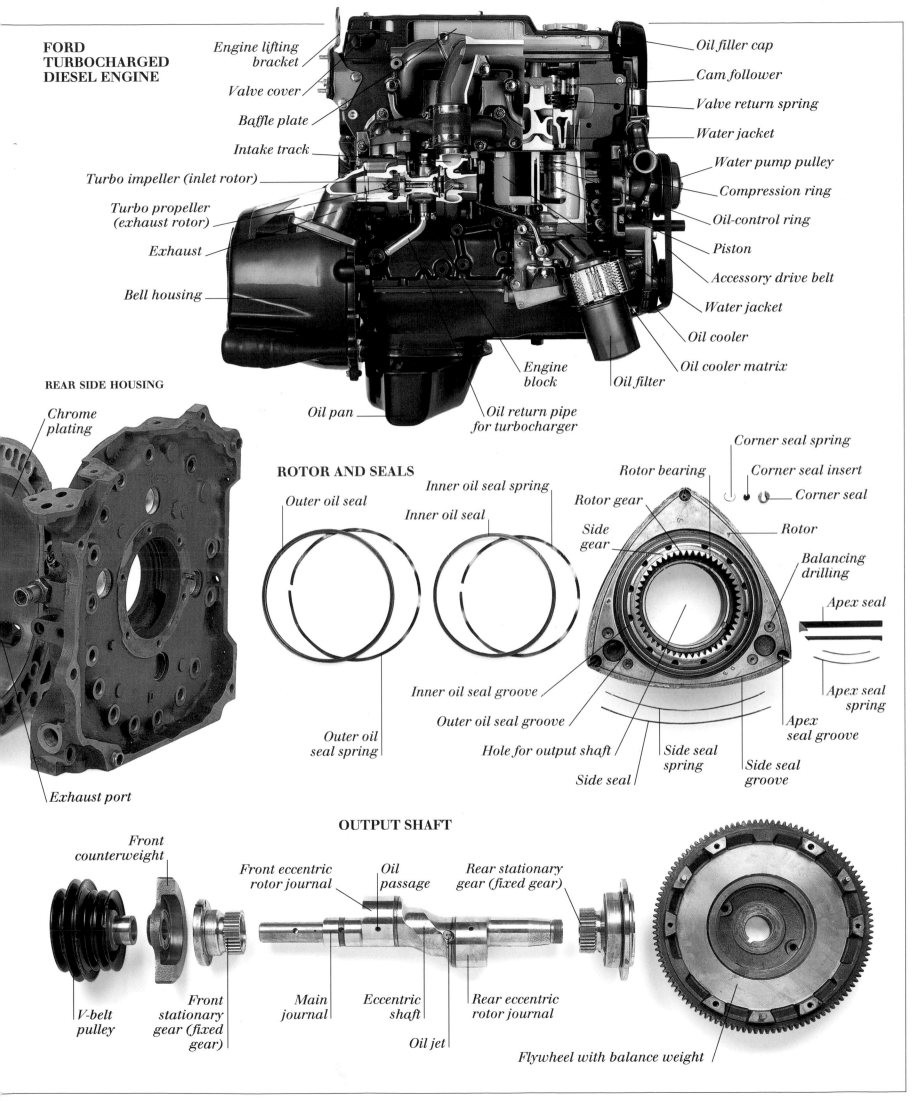

FORD TURBOCHARGED DIESEL ENGINE

Engine lifting bracket

Valve cover

Baffle plate

Intake track

Turbo impeller (inlet rotor)

Turbo propeller (exhaust rotor)

Exhaust

Bell housing

Oil filler cap

Cam follower

Valve return spring

Water jacket

Water pump pulley

Compression ring

Oil-control ring

Piston

Accessory drive belt

Water jacket

Oil cooler

Oil cooler matrix

Oil filter

Engine block

Oil pan

Oil return pipe for turbocharger

REAR SIDE HOUSING

Chrome plating

Exhaust port

ROTOR AND SEALS

Outer oil seal

Inner oil seal spring

Inner oil seal

Rotor bearing

Rotor gear

Side gear

Corner seal spring

Corner seal insert

Corner seal

Rotor

Balancing drilling

Apex seal

Apex seal spring

Inner oil seal groove

Outer oil seal groove

Outer oil seal spring

Hole for output shaft

Side seal spring

Side seal

Apex seal groove

Side seal groove

OUTPUT SHAFT

Front counterweight

Front eccentric rotor journal

Oil passage

Rear stationary gear (fixed gear)

V-belt pulley

Front stationary gear (fixed gear)

Main journal

Eccentric shaft

Oil jet

Rear eccentric rotor journal

Flywheel with balance weight

Carburetors

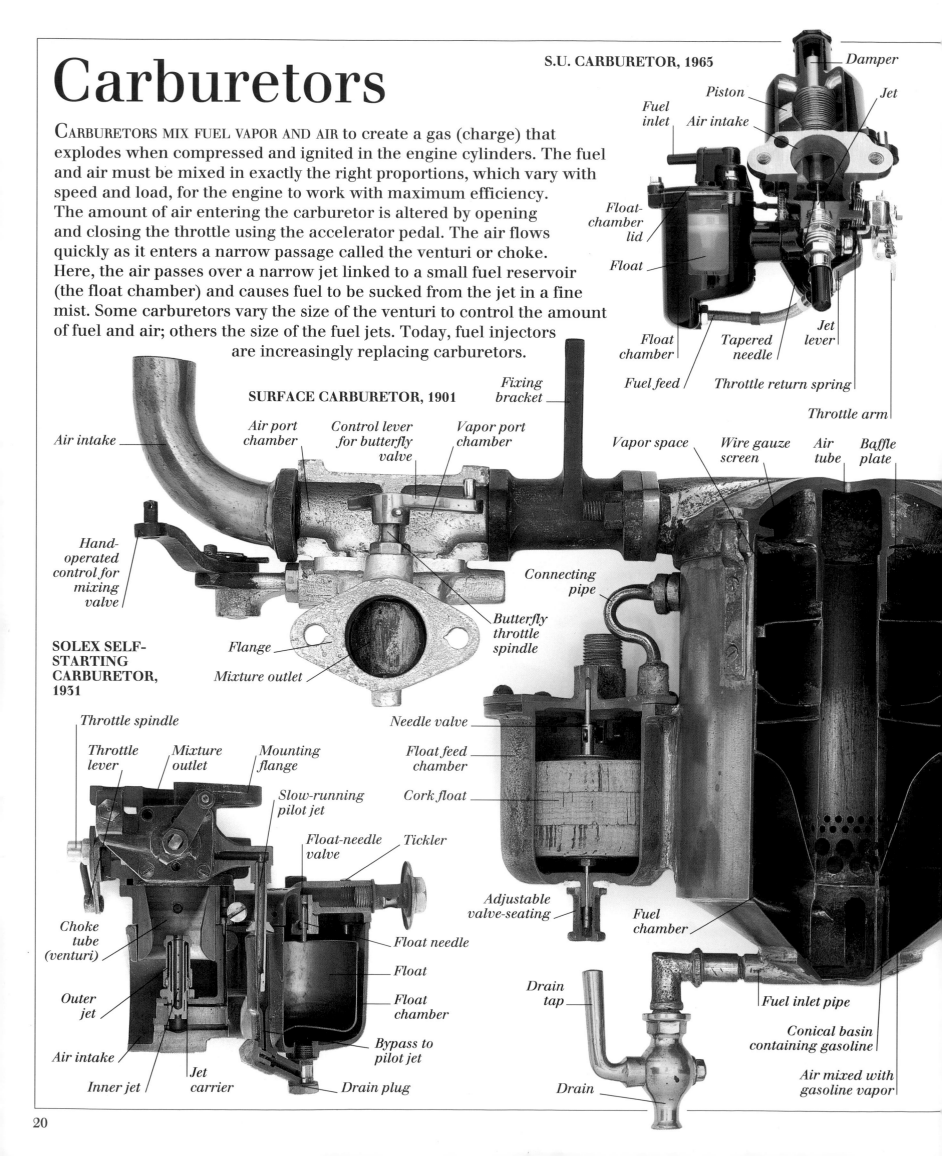

CARBURETORS MIX FUEL VAPOR AND AIR to create a gas (charge) that explodes when compressed and ignited in the engine cylinders. The fuel and air must be mixed in exactly the right proportions, which vary with speed and load, for the engine to work with maximum efficiency. The amount of air entering the carburetor is altered by opening and closing the throttle using the accelerator pedal. The air flows quickly as it enters a narrow passage called the venturi or choke. Here, the air passes over a narrow jet linked to a small fuel reservoir (the float chamber) and causes fuel to be sucked from the jet in a fine mist. Some carburetors vary the size of the venturi to control the amount of fuel and air; others the size of the fuel jets. Today, fuel injectors are increasingly replacing carburetors.

S.U. CARBURETOR, 1965

Damper

Piston

Jet

Fuel inlet

Air intake

Float-chamber lid

Float

Float chamber

Tapered needle

Jet lever

Fuel feed

Throttle return spring

Throttle arm

SURFACE CARBURETOR, 1901

Fixing bracket

Air intake

Air port chamber

Control lever for butterfly valve

Vapor port chamber

Vapor space

Wire gauze screen

Air tube

Baffle plate

Hand-operated control for mixing valve

Connecting pipe

Butterfly throttle spindle

Flange

Mixture outlet

SOLEX SELF-STARTING CARBURETOR, 1931

Throttle spindle

Throttle lever

Mixture outlet

Mounting flange

Slow-running pilot jet

Float-needle valve

Tickler

Choke tube (venturi)

Outer jet

Air intake

Inner jet

Jet carrier

Float needle

Float

Float chamber

Bypass to pilot jet

Drain plug

Needle valve

Float feed chamber

Cork float

Adjustable valve-seating

Fuel chamber

Drain tap

Drain

Fuel inlet pipe

Conical basin containing gasoline

Air mixed with gasoline vapor

20

WEBER TWIN CHOKE CARBURETOR, 1991

WEBER TWIN CHOKE CARBURETOR, 1991

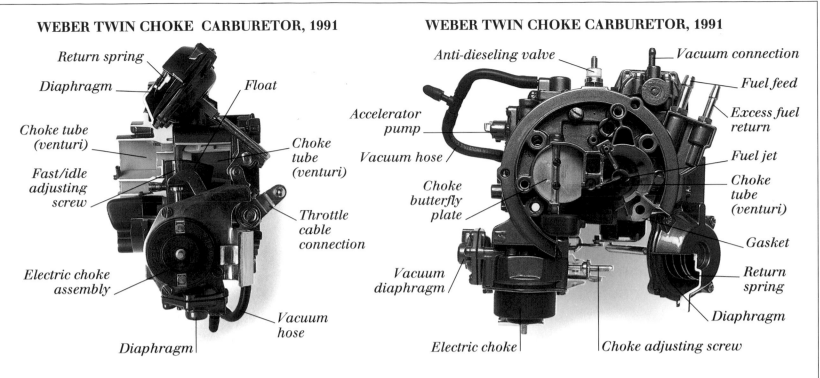

Return spring

Diaphragm

Float

Choke tube (venturi)

Choke tube (venturi)

Fast/idle adjusting screw

Throttle cable connection

Electric choke assembly

Vacuum hose

Diaphragm

Anti-dieseling valve

Vacuum connection

Fuel feed

Accelerator pump

Excess fuel return

Vacuum hose

Fuel jet

Choke butterfly plate

Choke tube (venturi)

Gasket

Vacuum diaphragm

Return spring

Diaphragm

Electric choke

Choke adjusting screw

SCOTT ROBINSON CARBURETOR, 1911

COX ATMOS CARBURETOR, 1918

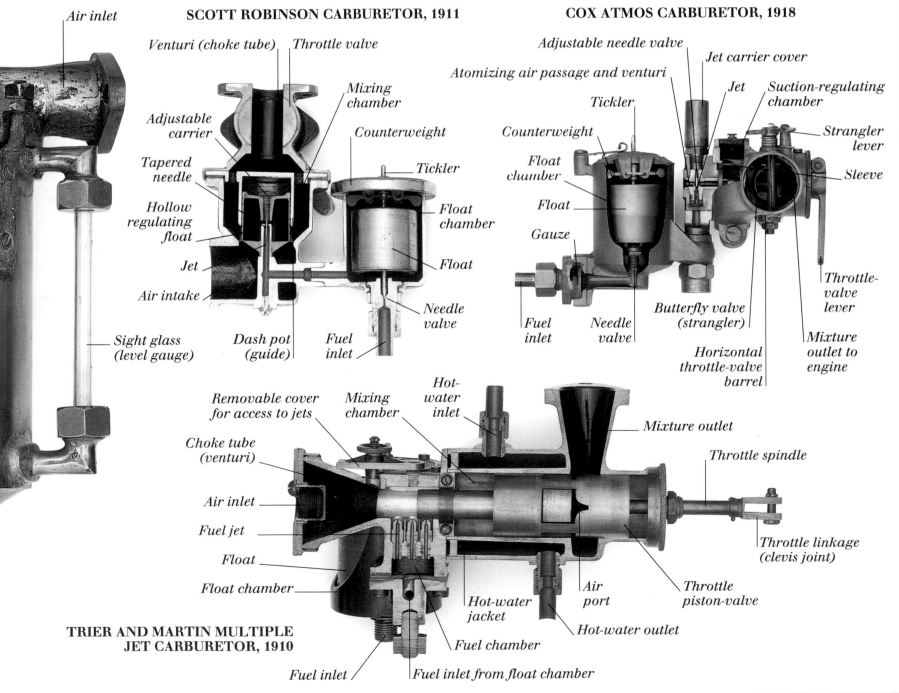

Air inlet

Venturi (choke tube)

Throttle valve

Mixing chamber

Adjustable carrier

Counterweight

Tapered needle

Tickler

Hollow regulating float

Float chamber

Jet

Float

Air intake

Needle valve

Sight glass (level gauge)

Dash pot (guide)

Fuel inlet

Adjustable needle valve

Jet carrier cover

Atomizing air passage and venturi

Jet

Suction-regulating chamber

Tickler

Counterweight

Strangler lever

Float chamber

Sleeve

Float

Gauze

Butterfly valve (strangler)

Throttle-valve lever

Fuel inlet

Needle valve

Horizontal throttle-valve barrel

Mixture outlet to engine

Removable cover for access to jets

Mixing chamber

Hot-water inlet

Mixture outlet

Choke tube (venturi)

Throttle spindle

Air inlet

Fuel jet

Throttle linkage (clevis joint)

Float

Float chamber

Air port

Throttle piston-valve

Hot-water jacket

Hot-water outlet

Fuel chamber

TRIER AND MARTIN MULTIPLE JET CARBURETOR, 1910

Fuel inlet

Fuel inlet from float chamber

Ignition systems

IGNITION OF THE FUEL/AIR MIXTURE in the engine must occur at precisely the moment of maximum compression to ensure the most efficient combustion. Some of the earliest cars used the crude method of red-hot platinum tubes heated by gasoline burners to ignite the mixture. Electric ignition soon took over: a distributor sent a carefully-timed electric current to each cylinder in turn, where the current jumped a gap between points in a spark plug, creating a spark to ignite the charge in the cylinder. Two favored methods of creating the current were the magneto, which generated a high-voltage electromagnetic current, and the coil, which amplified the voltage of a separate battery. Timing the spark might be performed mechanically by the distributor, or electronically by an electronic ignition system. The most modern systems use a computer to time the spark very precisely, allowing the engine to run at maximum efficiency.

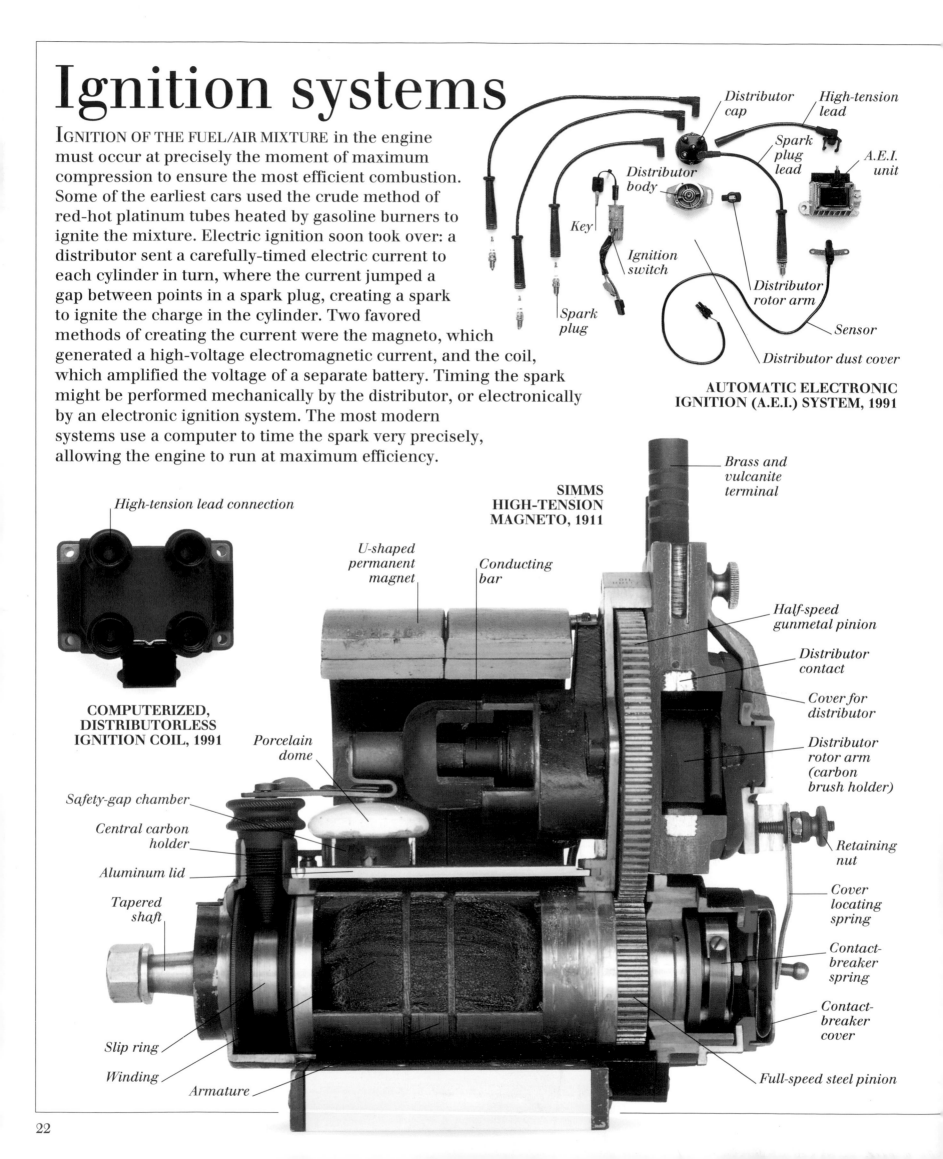

Distributor cap

High-tension lead

Spark plug lead

A.E.I. unit

Distributor body

Key

Ignition switch

Distributor rotor arm

Spark plug

Distributor dust cover

Sensor

AUTOMATIC ELECTRONIC IGNITION (A.E.I.) SYSTEM, 1991

High-tension lead connection

COMPUTERIZED, DISTRIBUTORLESS IGNITION COIL, 1991

SIMMS HIGH-TENSION MAGNETO, 1911

Brass and vulcanite terminal

U-shaped permanent magnet

Conducting bar

Half-speed gunmetal pinion

Distributor contact

Cover for distributor

Distributor rotor arm (carbon brush holder)

Porcelain dome

Safety-gap chamber

Central carbon holder

Aluminum lid

Tapered shaft

Retaining nut

Cover locating spring

Contact-breaker spring

Contact-breaker cover

Slip ring

Winding

Armature

Full-speed steel pinion

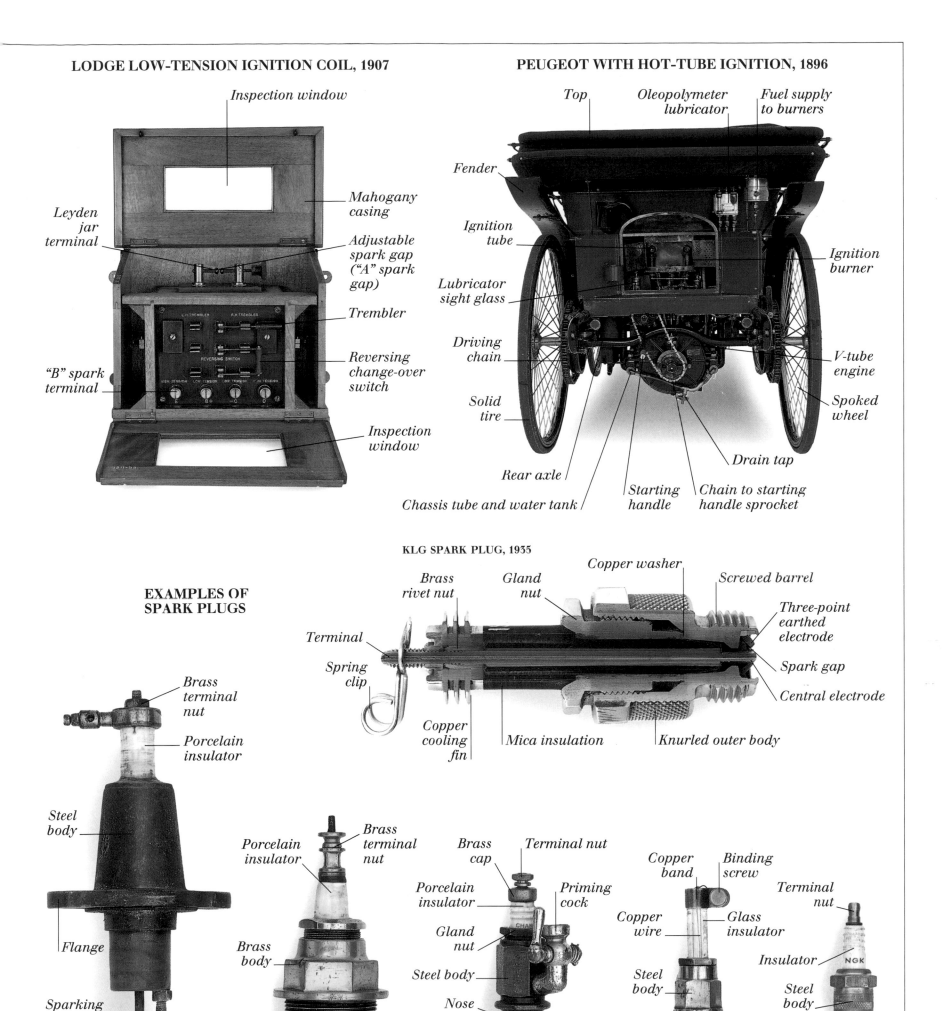

LODGE LOW-TENSION IGNITION COIL, 1907

Inspection window

Leyden jar terminal

Mahogany casing

Adjustable spark gap ("A" spark gap)

Trembler

Reversing change-over switch

"B" spark terminal

Inspection window

PEUGEOT WITH HOT-TUBE IGNITION, 1896

Top

Oleopolymeter lubricator

Fuel supply to burners

Fender

Ignition tube

Ignition burner

Lubricator sight glass

Driving chain

V-tube engine

Solid tire

Spoked wheel

Drain tap

Rear axle

Starting handle

Chain to starting handle sprocket

Chassis tube and water tank

KLG SPARK PLUG, 1935

Brass rivet nut

Gland nut

Copper washer

Screwed barrel

Terminal

Three-point earthed electrode

Spring clip

Spark gap

Central electrode

Copper cooling fin

Mica insulation

Knurled outer body

EXAMPLES OF SPARK PLUGS

Brass terminal nut

Porcelain insulator

Steel body

Flange

Sparking point

Earthed electrode

BENZ PLUG, 1888

Porcelain insulator

Brass terminal nut

Brass body

Earthed electrode

Sparking point

DELAHAYE PLUG, 1901

Brass cap

Terminal nut

Porcelain insulator

Priming cock

Gland nut

Steel body

Nose

Earthed electrode

Sparking point

CHAMPION PRIMING PLUG, c.1920

Copper band

Binding screw

Copper wire

Glass insulator

Steel body

Nose

Platinum sparking point

GLASS-INSULATED PLUG, 1936

Terminal nut

Insulator

Steel body

NGK NON-DETACHABLE PLUG, c.1963

23

Power boosters

AN ENGINE'S POWER OUTPUT can be increased by forcing more of the fuel/air mixture (the charge) into the cylinders (forced induction) to provide a bigger explosion on the power stroke. There are two types of forced induction: supercharging and turbocharging. A supercharger, or blower, uses rotating vanes or lobes to force air into the engine; the increased flow of air sucks (or blows) more fuel vapor in, increasing the charge in the cylinders. Superchargers are mechanically driven by the engine, using some of its power. Turbochargers do the same job but are driven by exhaust gases, so they don't use any of the engine's power. The power and efficiency of an engine can also be increased by fuel injectors, which have regulators that react to the engine's requirements by injecting exactly the right amount of fuel.

AIR AND GAS FLOW IN A TURBOCHARGER FOR A MODERN V6 ENGINE

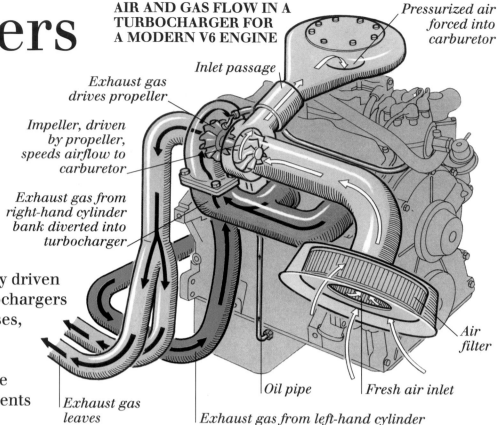

Pressurized air forced into carburetor

Inlet passage

Exhaust gas drives propeller

Impeller, driven by propeller, speeds airflow to carburetor

Exhaust gas from right-hand cylinder bank diverted into turbocharger

Air filter

Oil pipe

Fresh air inlet

Exhaust gas leaves turbocharger

Exhaust gas from left-hand cylinder bank diverted into turbocharger

PARTS OF A SUPERCHARGER, c.1948

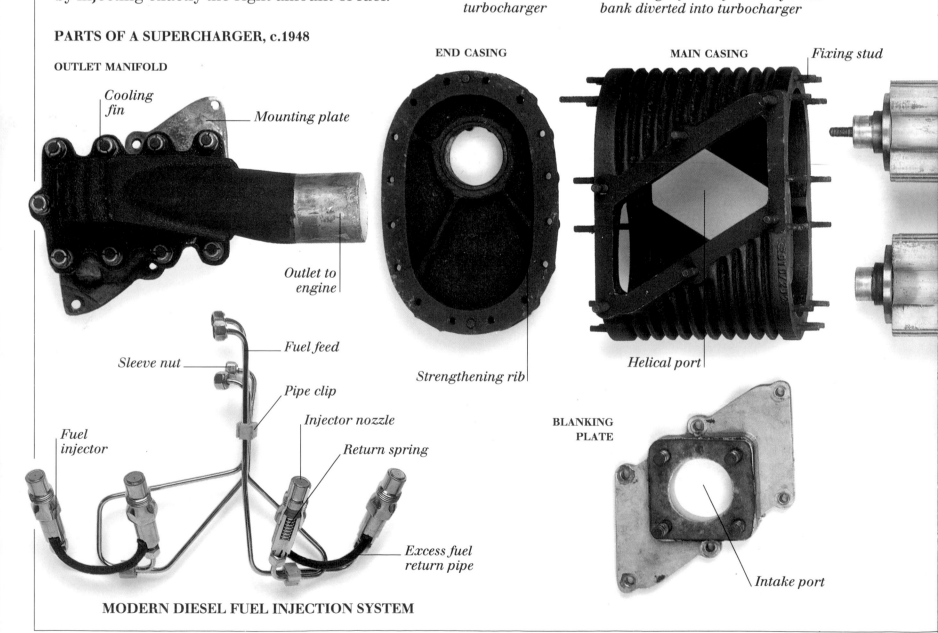

OUTLET MANIFOLD

Cooling fin

Mounting plate

Outlet to engine

END CASING

Strengthening rib

MAIN CASING

Fixing stud

Helical port

Sleeve nut

Fuel feed

Pipe clip

Injector nozzle

Return spring

Fuel injector

BLANKING PLATE

Excess fuel return pipe

Intake port

MODERN DIESEL FUEL INJECTION SYSTEM

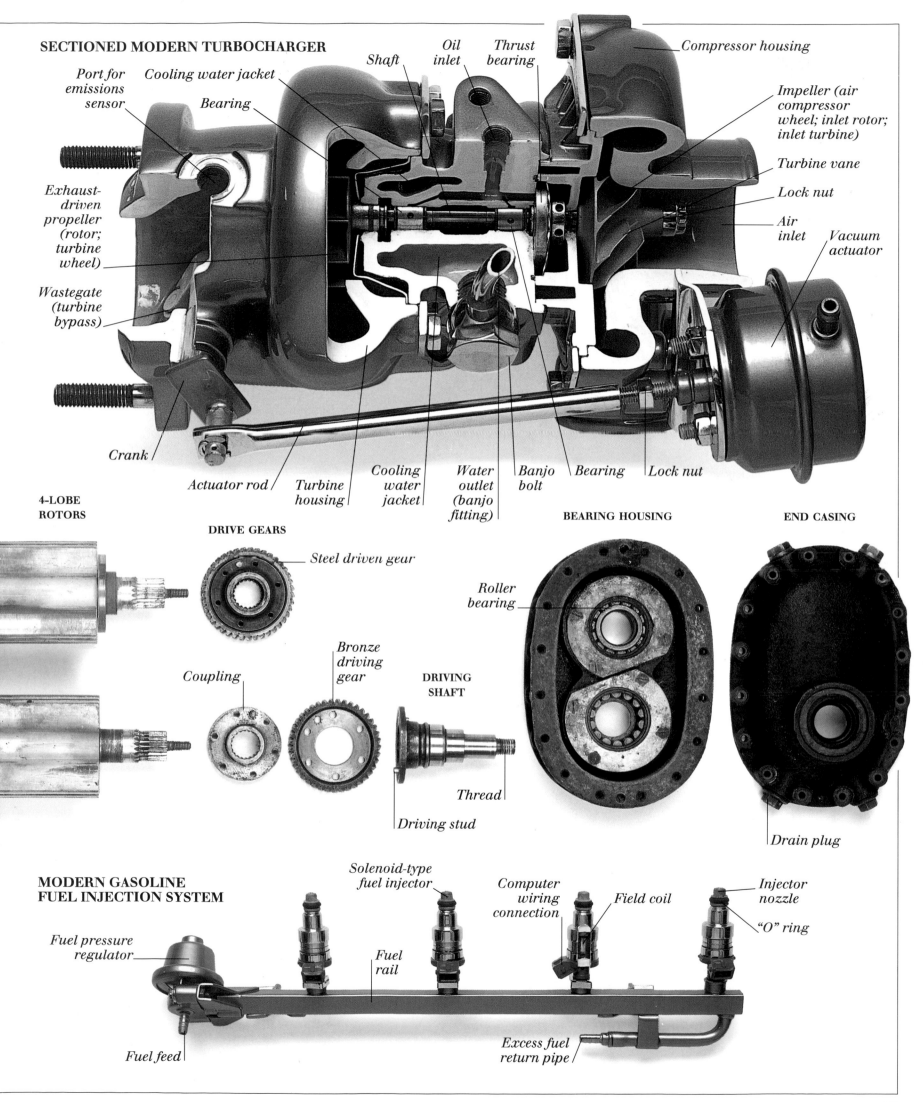

SECTIONED MODERN TURBOCHARGER

Port for emissions sensor

Cooling water jacket

Bearing

Shaft

Oil inlet

Thrust bearing

Compressor housing

Impeller (air compressor wheel; inlet rotor; inlet turbine)

Turbine vane

Lock nut

Air inlet

Vacuum actuator

Exhaust-driven propeller (rotor; turbine wheel)

Wastegate (turbine bypass)

Crank

Actuator rod

Turbine housing

Cooling water jacket

Water outlet (banjo fitting)

Banjo bolt

Bearing

Lock nut

4-LOBE ROTORS

DRIVE GEARS

Steel driven gear

Coupling

Bronze driving gear

DRIVING SHAFT

Thread

Driving stud

BEARING HOUSING

Roller bearing

END CASING

Drain plug

MODERN GASOLINE FUEL INJECTION SYSTEM

Solenoid-type fuel injector

Computer wiring connection

Field coil

Injector nozzle

"O" ring

Fuel pressure regulator

Fuel rail

Fuel feed

Excess fuel return pipe

25

Cooling and lubrication

COMBUSTION TEMPERATURES in an engine's cylinders can reach around 3,000°F (1,700°C), enough heat to melt the cylinder head. To prevent this, most cars have a water-cooling system, although a few cars use air-cooling. Coolant (water mixed with antifreeze) is circulated around a jacket surrounding the cylinders, then to a radiator, where the heat the coolant has absorbed is released into the air. Some heat may be used to warm the car's interior. Modern vehicles increasingly use separate air-conditioning systems to maintain a steady temperature. Oil lubrication also cools the engine, but its main role is to maintain a thin film of oil between moving parts to prevent wearing and seizing. Most lubrication systems circulate oil from a sump attached to the engine. The dry sump lubrication system, used in some competition cars, keeps oil in a separate tank to prevent the oil from overheating.

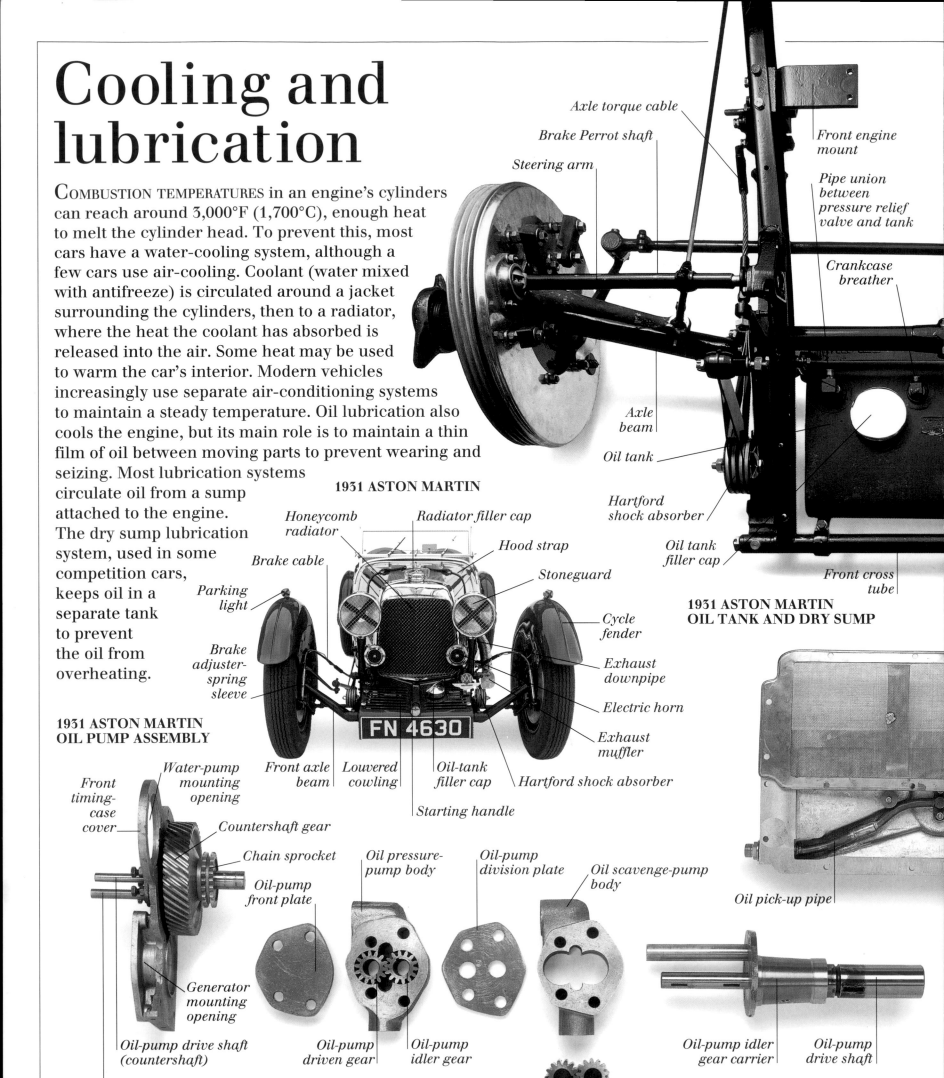

1931 ASTON MARTIN

1931 ASTON MARTIN OIL TANK AND DRY SUMP

1931 ASTON MARTIN OIL PUMP ASSEMBLY

- Axle torque cable
- Brake Perrot shaft
- Steering arm
- Front engine mount
- Pipe union between pressure relief valve and tank
- Crankcase breather
- Axle beam
- Oil tank
- Hartford shock absorber
- Oil tank filler cap
- Front cross tube

- Honeycomb radiator
- Radiator filler cap
- Hood strap
- Brake cable
- Stoneguard
- Parking light
- Cycle fender
- Brake adjuster-spring sleeve
- Exhaust downpipe
- Electric horn
- Exhaust muffler
- FN 4630
- Front axle beam
- Louvered cowling
- Oil-tank filler cap
- Hartford shock absorber
- Starting handle

- Front timing-case cover
- Water-pump mounting opening
- Countershaft gear
- Chain sprocket
- Oil-pump front plate
- Oil pressure-pump body
- Oil-pump division plate
- Oil scavenge-pump body
- Oil pick-up pipe
- Generator mounting opening
- Oil-pump drive shaft (countershaft)
- Oil-pump driven gear
- Oil-pump idler gear
- Oil-pump idler gear carrier
- Oil-pump drive shaft
- Oil-pump idler gear carrier
- Oil-pump driven gear
- Oil-pump idler gear

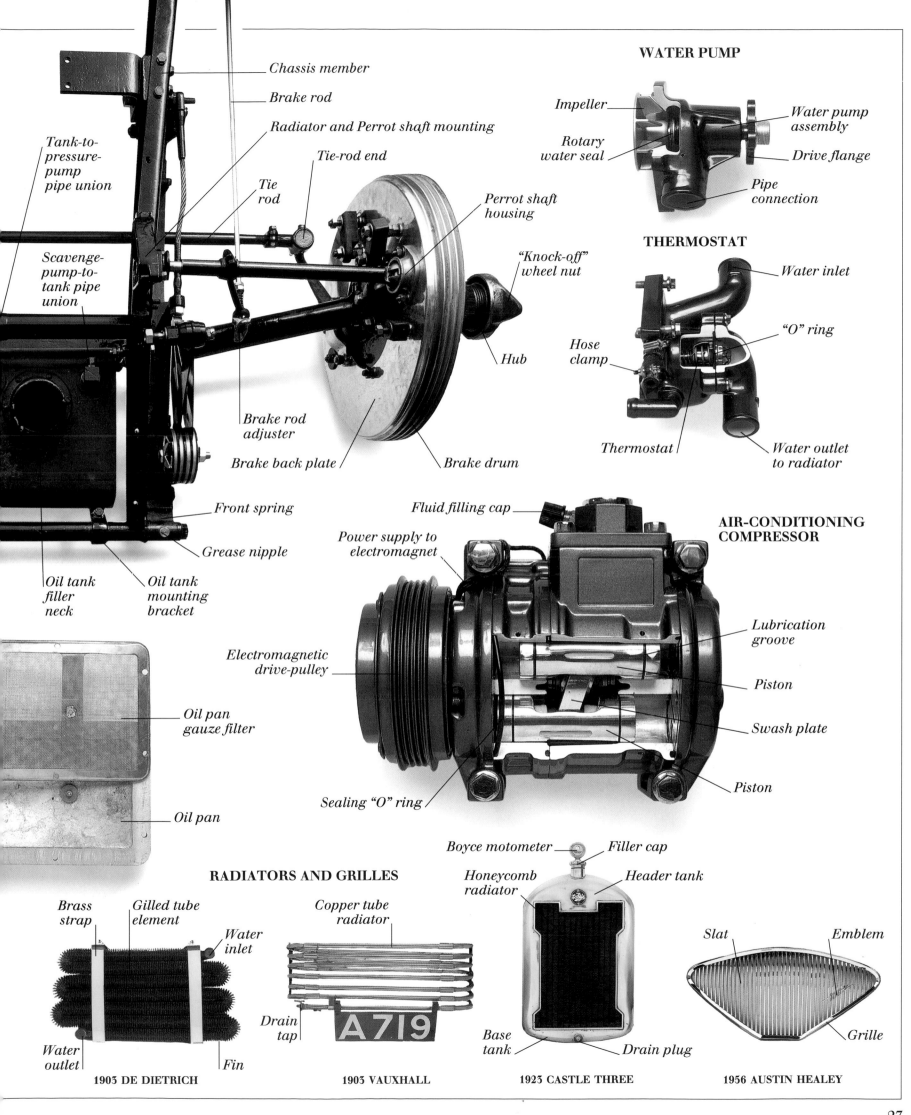

Chassis member

Brake rod

Radiator and Perrot shaft mounting

Tie-rod end

Tie rod

Tank-to-pressure-pump pipe union

Perrot shaft housing

Scavenge-pump-to-tank pipe union

"Knock-off" wheel nut

Hub

Brake rod adjuster

Brake back plate

Brake drum

Front spring

Grease nipple

Oil tank filler neck

Oil tank mounting bracket

WATER PUMP

Impeller

Rotary water seal

Water pump assembly

Drive flange

Pipe connection

THERMOSTAT

Water inlet

"O" ring

Hose clamp

Thermostat

Water outlet to radiator

AIR-CONDITIONING COMPRESSOR

Fluid filling cap

Power supply to electromagnet

Lubrication groove

Piston

Electromagnetic drive-pulley

Swash plate

Piston

Sealing "O" ring

Oil pan gauze filter

Oil pan

RADIATORS AND GRILLES

Boyce motometer

Filler cap

Honeycomb radiator

Header tank

Brass strap

Gilled tube element

Copper tube radiator

Water inlet

Slat

Emblem

Drain tap

A 719

Base tank

Drain plug

Grille

Water outlet

Fin

1903 DE DIETRICH

1903 VAUXHALL

1923 CASTLE THREE

1956 AUSTIN HEALEY

Clutch and gearbox

THE GEARBOX TRANSMITS POWER from the engine to the road wheels. It also allows the wheels to turn at different speeds to the engine. Modern gearboxes contain five or six sets of intermeshed cogs (including a reverse gear set) to apply the turning force of the engine (torque) most efficiently over as wide a range of road speeds as possible and to enable the car to climb hills. To engage gears, or to remain stationary with the engine running, the engine must be disconnected from the gearbox. This is achieved by the clutch, which has one plate connected to the engine (the driving plate) and another connected to the gearbox (the driven plate). To disconnect the engine from the gearbox, the clutch plates are unclamped so that they are no longer in contact; for the engine to drive the wheels, strong springs clamp the plates together.

MODERN FRICTION CLUTCH ASSEMBLY

PRESSURE PLATE (DRIVING PLATE)

Leaf spring

DRIVEN PLATE

Rivet

Heat-resistant lining

FLYWHEEL

Crankshaft bolt hole

Gearbox spline (input shaft)

Starting motor ring gear

Clutch plate mounting hole

Clutch release rod

Clutch bell-housing

MODERN 5-SPEED MANUAL GEARBOX

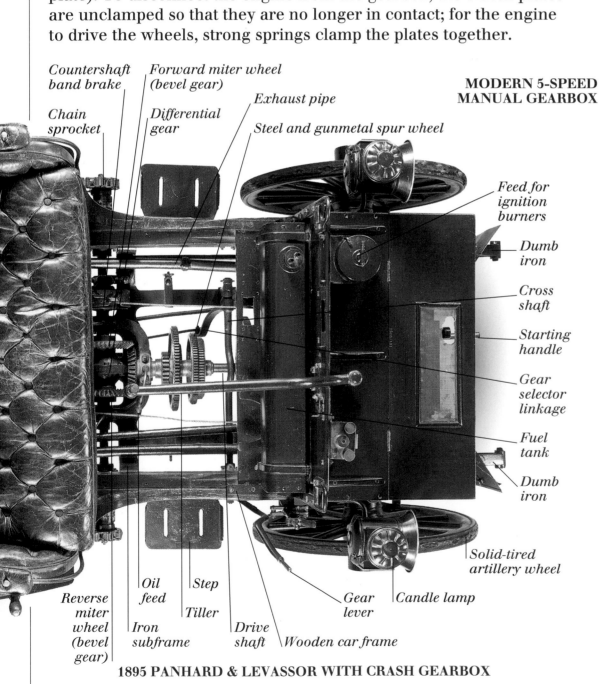

Countershaft band brake

Forward miter wheel (bevel gear)

Exhaust pipe

Chain sprocket

Differential gear

Steel and gunmetal spur wheel

Feed for ignition burners

Dumb iron

Cross shaft

Starting handle

Gear selector linkage

Fuel tank

Dumb iron

Solid-tired artillery wheel

Reverse miter wheel (bevel gear)

Oil feed

Step

Tiller

Iron subframe

Drive shaft

Wooden car frame

Gear lever

Candle lamp

1895 PANHARD & LEVASSOR WITH CRASH GEARBOX

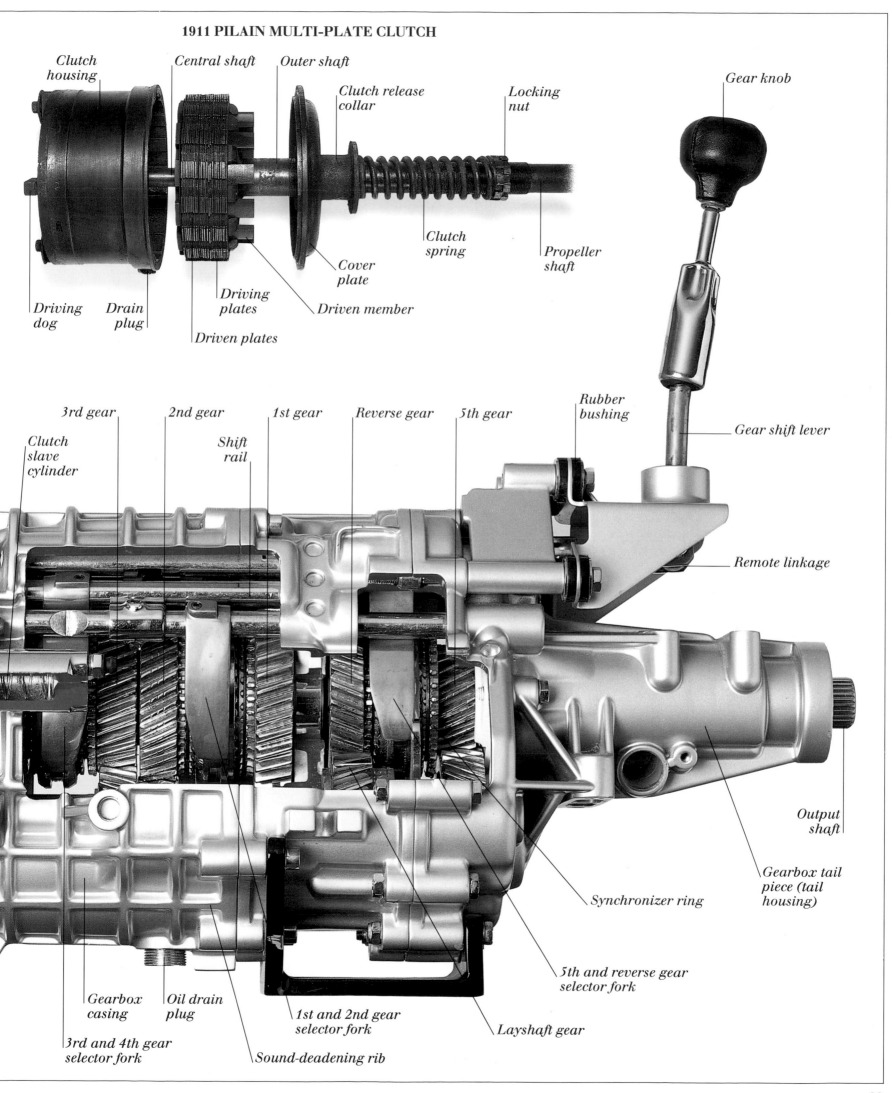

1911 PILAIN MULTI-PLATE CLUTCH

Clutch housing

Central shaft

Outer shaft

Clutch release collar

Locking nut

Gear knob

Clutch spring

Propeller shaft

Cover plate

Driven member

Driving plates

Driven plates

Driving dog

Drain plug

3rd gear

2nd gear

1st gear

Reverse gear

5th gear

Rubber bushing

Gear shift lever

Clutch slave cylinder

Shift rail

Remote linkage

Output shaft

Gearbox tail piece (tail housing)

Synchronizer ring

5th and reverse gear selector fork

Gearbox casing

Oil drain plug

1st and 2nd gear selector fork

Layshaft gear

3rd and 4th gear selector fork

Sound-deadening rib

Transmission systems

THE TRANSMISSION SYSTEM transmits the engine's power to the wheels. Early cars used chains or belts to achieve this. Modern cars use a clutch, gearbox, and drive shafts. Some modern cars have a continuously variable transmission, in which a belt runs between pulleys that expand and contract automatically to provide the right gearing ratio. The most common type of automatic gearbox contains planetary gear sets that are selected according to engine speed and throttle opening. Perhaps the most unusual form of transmission was that of the French Leyat, which had no clutch, gearbox, or final drive but was powered by a variable-speed propeller.

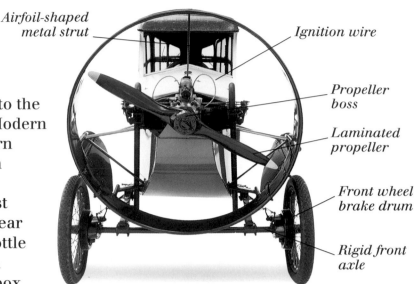

FRONT VIEW OF LEYAT, c.1924

Airfoil-shaped metal strut

Ignition wire

Propeller boss

Laminated propeller

Front wheel brake drum

Rigid front axle

SIDE VIEW OF LEYAT

Fuselage

Rear fender

Steering cabane

Beaded edge tire

Propeller shield (airscrew shield)

Flat twin engine

Wire wheel

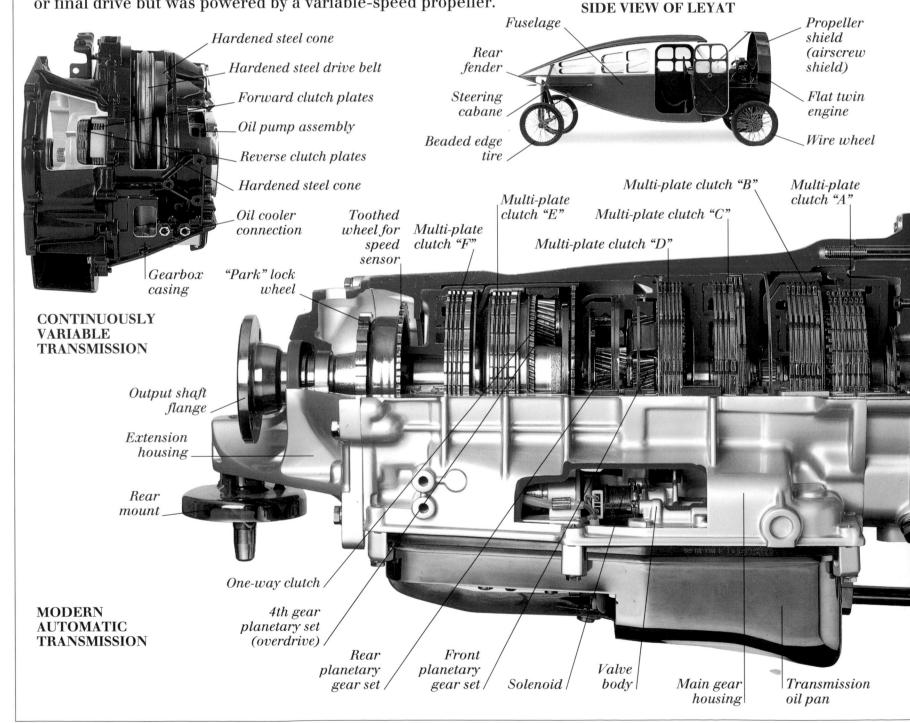

CONTINUOUSLY VARIABLE TRANSMISSION

Hardened steel cone

Hardened steel drive belt

Forward clutch plates

Oil pump assembly

Reverse clutch plates

Hardened steel cone

Oil cooler connection

Gearbox casing

MODERN AUTOMATIC TRANSMISSION

Toothed wheel for speed sensor

"Park" lock wheel

Output shaft flange

Extension housing

Rear mount

One-way clutch

4th gear planetary set (overdrive)

Rear planetary gear set

Front planetary gear set

Solenoid

Multi-plate clutch "F"

Multi-plate clutch "E"

Multi-plate clutch "D"

Multi-plate clutch "C"

Multi-plate clutch "B"

Multi-plate clutch "A"

Valve body

Main gear housing

Transmission oil pan

CHAIN-DRIVEN 70-HP MERCEDES, 1904

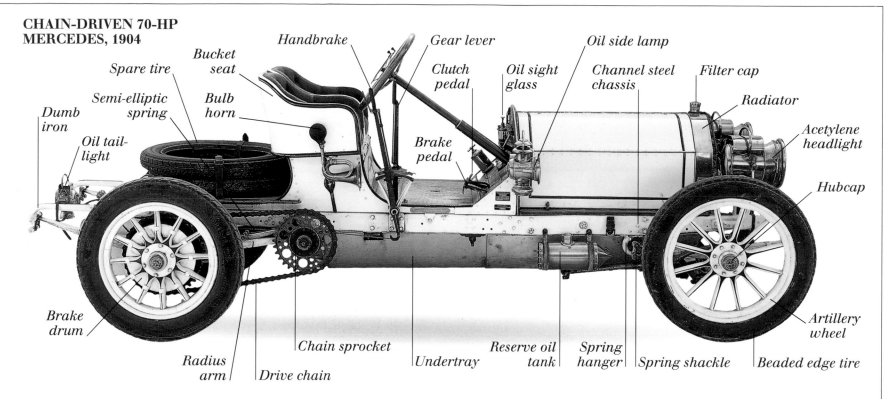

Handbrake
Gear lever
Oil side lamp
Filter cap
Bucket seat
Clutch pedal
Oil sight glass
Channel steel chassis
Radiator
Spare tire
Bulb horn
Acetylene headlight
Semi-elliptic spring
Dumb iron
Oil tail-light
Brake pedal
Hubcap
Brake drum
Radius arm
Drive chain
Chain sprocket
Undertray
Reserve oil tank
Spring hanger
Spring shackle
Beaded edge tire
Artillery wheel

BELT-DRIVEN DAIMLER MAYBACH, 1895

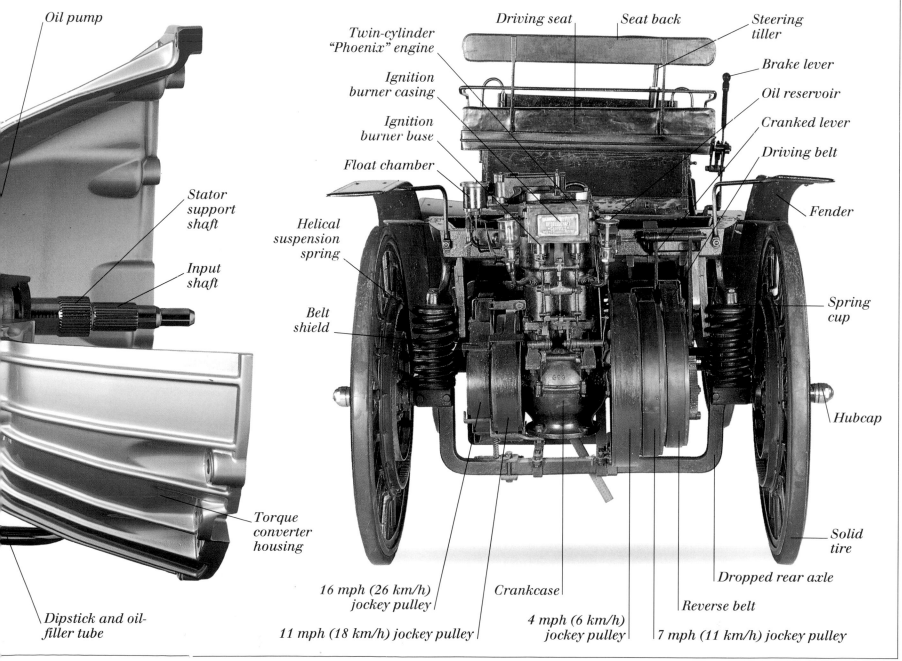

Oil pump
Driving seat
Seat back
Steering tiller
Twin-cylinder "Phoenix" engine
Brake lever
Ignition burner casing
Oil reservoir
Stator support shaft
Ignition burner base
Cranked lever
Input shaft
Float chamber
Driving belt
Fender
Helical suspension spring
Belt shield
Spring cup
Hubcap
Torque converter housing
Dipstick and oil-filler tube
16 mph (26 km/h) jockey pulley
Crankcase
Reverse belt
Solid tire
Dropped rear axle
11 mph (18 km/h) jockey pulley
4 mph (6 km/h) jockey pulley
7 mph (11 km/h) jockey pulley

Final drive and steering

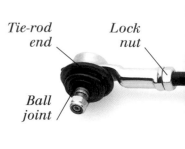

Drive shaft

Gearbox

MOST EARLY CARS USED THE PANHARD transmission system, named after the manufacturer René Panhard, in which a front-mounted engine drove the rear wheels through a multiple-ratio gearbox. Since the late 1950s in Europe, and the early 1970s in the United States, most cars have used front-wheel drive. Today, powerful cars increasingly use four-wheel drive for its better road-holding. Whatever the drive system used, a driven axle is turned by a final-drive gear, usually located in the gearbox in front-wheel-drive cars. The final-drive gear incorporates a differential gear that allows the outer wheel to turn faster than the inner when driving around corners. In most cars, only the front wheels are steered. The steering column is joined by a pinion to a rack. When the steering wheel is turned, the pinion rolls the rack either right or left, so turning the wheels. Some cars have power-assisted steering, in which hydraulic power makes it easier for the driver to turn the steering wheel. A few cars have steering on all four wheels. The four-wheel-steering rack shown here an electronic control unit that controls the direction of the rear wheels, while the front wheels are steered conventionally.

FRONT VIEW OF A FOUR-WHEEL-DRIVE RENAULT ESPACE

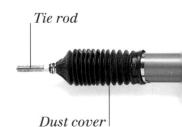

Tie-rod end

Lock nut

Ball joint

Tie rod

Dust cover

Drive shaft

FOUR-WHEEL-DRIVE RUNNING GEAR

Aerodynamic windshield

"Monobox" body

Rear axle

SIDE VIEW OF A FOUR-WHEEL-DRIVE RENAULT ESPACE

Differential gear unit

Drive shaft

Brake assembly

DIFFERENTIAL UNIT

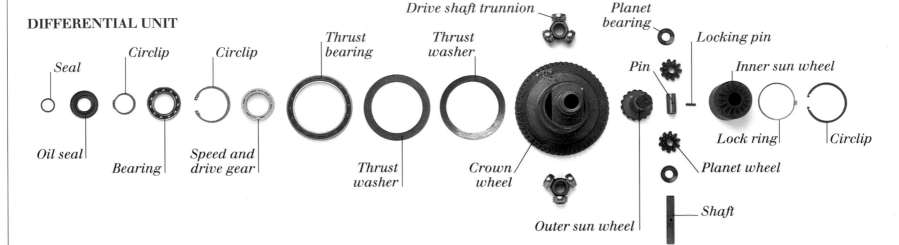

Seal

Circlip

Circlip

Thrust bearing

Thrust washer

Drive shaft trunnion

Planet bearing

Locking pin

Pin

Inner sun wheel

Oil seal

Bearing

Speed and drive gear

Thrust washer

Crown wheel

Lock ring

Planet wheel

Circlip

Shaft

Outer sun wheel

32

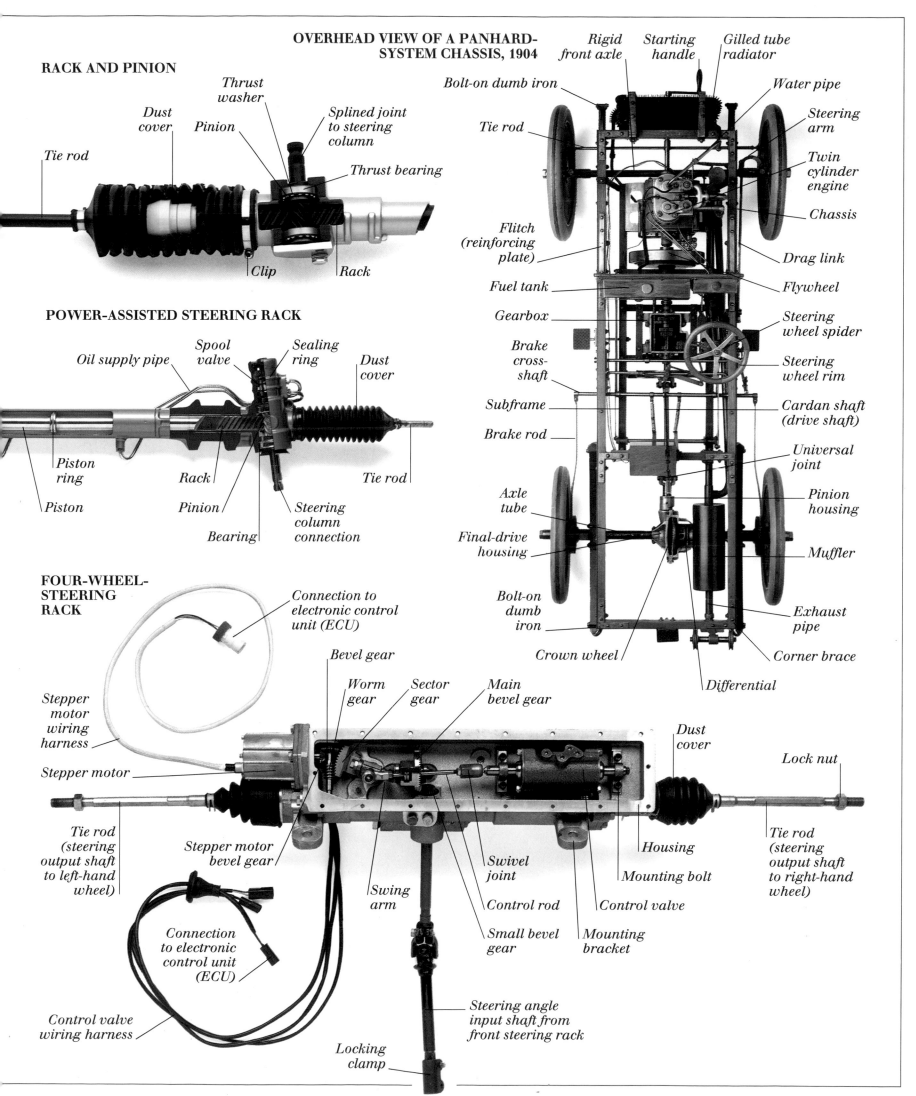

RACK AND PINION

Tie rod
Dust cover
Pinion
Thrust washer
Splined joint to steering column
Thrust bearing
Clip
Rack

OVERHEAD VIEW OF A PANHARD-SYSTEM CHASSIS, 1904

Rigid front axle
Starting handle
Gilled tube radiator
Bolt-on dumb iron
Water pipe
Tie rod
Steering arm
Twin cylinder engine
Chassis
Flitch (reinforcing plate)
Drag link
Fuel tank
Flywheel
Gearbox
Steering wheel spider
Brake cross-shaft
Steering wheel rim
Subframe
Cardan shaft (drive shaft)
Brake rod
Universal joint
Axle tube
Pinion housing
Final-drive housing
Muffler
Bolt-on dumb iron
Exhaust pipe
Crown wheel
Corner brace
Differential

POWER-ASSISTED STEERING RACK

Spool valve
Sealing ring
Oil supply pipe
Dust cover
Piston ring
Rack
Tie rod
Piston
Pinion
Bearing
Steering column connection

FOUR-WHEEL-STEERING RACK

Connection to electronic control unit (ECU)
Bevel gear
Worm gear
Sector gear
Main bevel gear
Dust cover
Stepper motor wiring harness
Lock nut
Stepper motor
Tie rod (steering output shaft to left-hand wheel)
Stepper motor bevel gear
Swing arm
Swivel joint
Control rod
Small bevel gear
Control valve
Housing
Mounting bolt
Tie rod (steering output shaft to right-hand wheel)
Connection to electronic control unit (ECU)
Mounting bracket
Control valve wiring harness
Steering angle input shaft from front steering rack
Locking clamp

Suspension

TWIN TRAILING ARM INDEPENDENT FRONT SUSPENSION

SUSPENSION CUSHIONS THE CAR from the effects of irregular road surfaces. It also helps to maintain maximum contact between the tires and the road, and so is necessary for effective steering, braking, and acceleration. The earliest suspension systems —leaf springs made of layers of steel leaves—are still used in some cars. Most modern cars use coil springs, which, unlike leaf springs, have no built-in damping to eliminate unwanted bouncing over rough surfaces. Coil springs require separate hydraulic or gas-filled shock absorbers to counteract this bouncing. The MacPherson strut is an independent system that combines shock absorbers and a king pin (which acts as a bearing for the steering movement) in one unit. The de Dion rear suspension system was invented a century ago, but is still used in some modern sports cars because it reduces wheel spin and gives better road-holding.

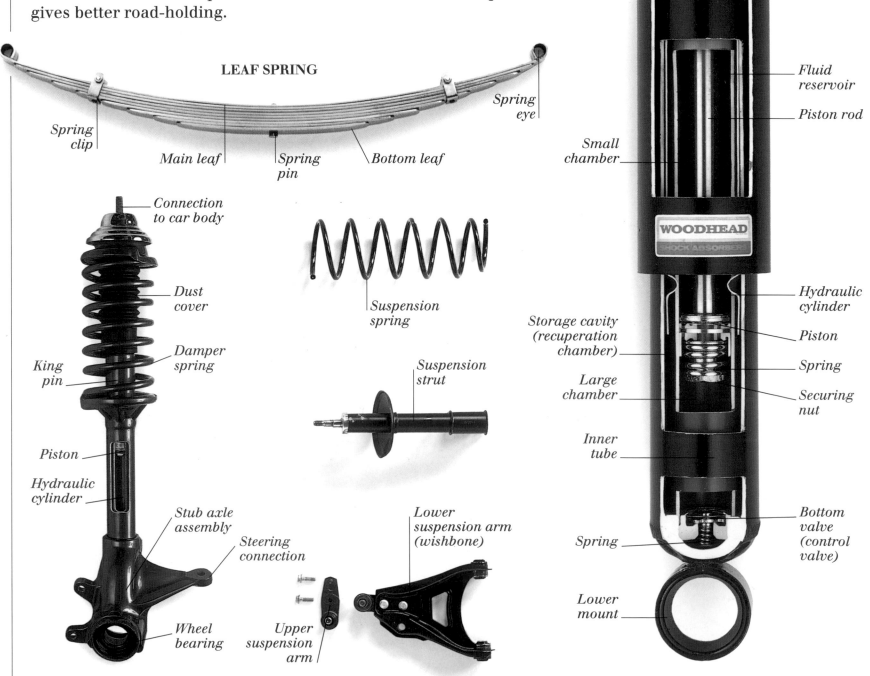

TELESCOPIC HYDRAULIC SHOCK ABSORBER, 1967

Chassis attachment eye (upper mount)

Outer tube

Fluid reservoir

Piston rod

Small chamber

Hydraulic cylinder

Storage cavity (recuperation chamber)

Piston

Large chamber

Spring

Securing nut

Inner tube

Spring

Bottom valve (control valve)

Lower mount

LEAF SPRING

Spring eye

Spring clip

Main leaf

Spring pin

Bottom leaf

Connection to car body

Dust cover

King pin

Damper spring

Piston

Hydraulic cylinder

Stub axle assembly

Steering connection

Wheel bearing

Upper suspension arm

Suspension spring

Suspension strut

Lower suspension arm (wishbone)

MACPHERSON STRUT

COIL AND WISHBONE SUSPENSION

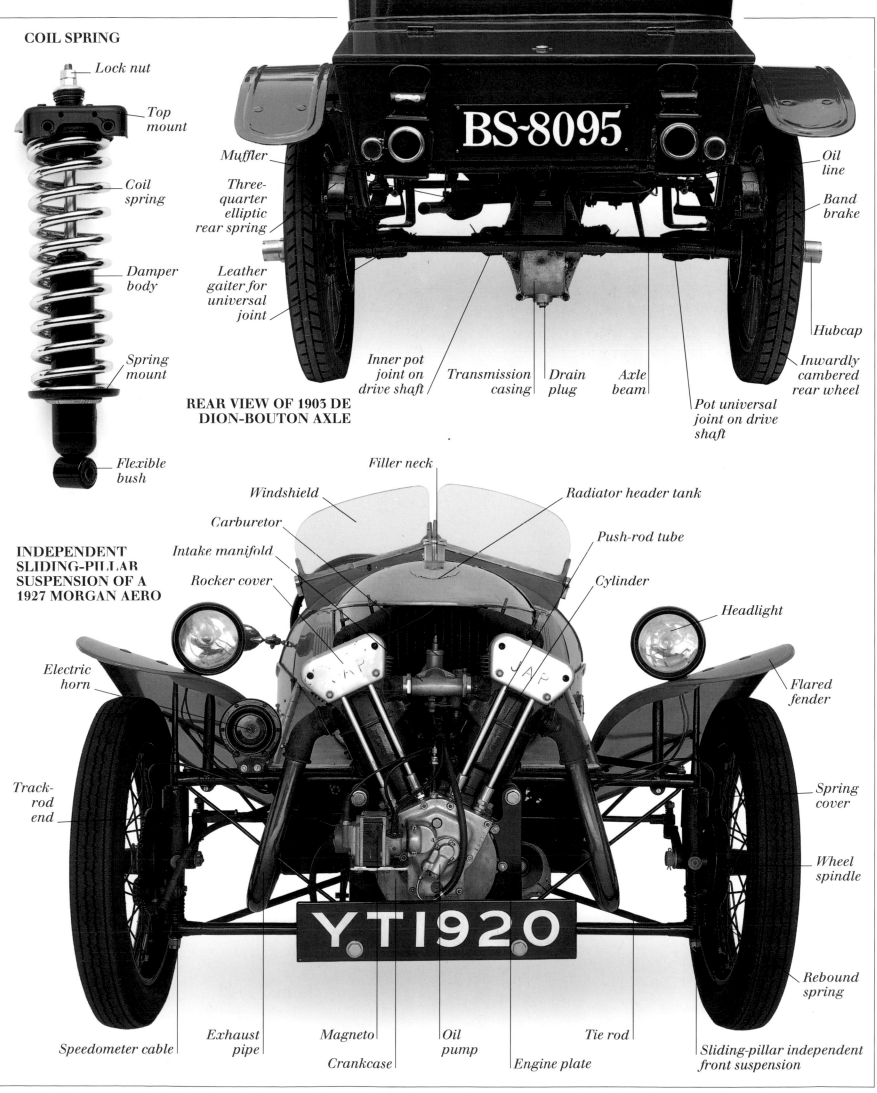

COIL SPRING

Lock nut

Top mount

Coil spring

Damper body

Spring mount

Flexible bush

Muffler

Three-quarter elliptic rear spring

Leather gaiter for universal joint

REAR VIEW OF 1903 DE DION-BOUTON AXLE

Inner pot joint on drive shaft

Transmission casing

Drain plug

Axle beam

Pot universal joint on drive shaft

Oil line

Band brake

Hubcap

Inwardly cambered rear wheel

INDEPENDENT SLIDING-PILLAR SUSPENSION OF A 1927 MORGAN AERO

Filler neck

Windshield

Carburetor

Intake manifold

Rocker cover

Radiator header tank

Push-rod tube

Cylinder

Headlight

Electric horn

Flared fender

Track-rod end

Spring cover

Wheel spindle

Rebound spring

Speedometer cable

Exhaust pipe

Crankcase

Magneto

Oil pump

Engine plate

Tie rod

Sliding-pillar independent front suspension

Wheels and tires

IT IS NOT ENOUGH FOR A CAR WHEEL SIMPLY TO BE ROUND; it must also be strong enough to withstand violent stresses and carefully balanced so that it rotates evenly. It must be light yet stiff so that it does not affect the steering and suspension, and must allow air to flow over and cool the brakes. Early cars had wooden-spoked wheels, as did horse-drawn carriages, but such wheels can be distorted by heavy loads and by shrinkage. Wire wheels, derived from bicycle wheels, effectively hang the car from the wheel rim by precisely-tensioned thin spokes. The simplest form of modern wheel is the pressed steel disc, while cast aluminium wheels permit wider (low-profile) tires to be fitted for better grip (see pp. 46-47). The first tires were made from solid rubber but they were superseded by pneumatic (air-filled) tires, which provided a more comfortable ride.

A major advance came with the introduction of radial-ply tires in the 1950s—their flexible sidewalls give better cornering and longer tread life.

HUB

Bolt-on plate

Spoke hole

Splines / Thread / "Knock-off" nut

Dowel

Rounded tongue to enter felloe

Belly

Face of spoke

Knock

Spoke

Felloe

Bolt hole for hub

Ring of felloes

Hole for spoke

ARTILLERY WHEEL (WOODEN-SPOKED WHEEL)

"BIBENDUM," TRADEMARK OF THE MICHELIN TIRE COMPANY

MICHELIN

TYPES OF TIRE

EXTRA-FORT, ITALY, 1911

METAL-STUDDED NON-SKID, ITALY, 1914

RUBBER-STUDDED, FRANCE, 1926

CONFORT BIBENDUM, FRANCE, 1928

CABLE, ITALY, 1919

TEXTILE-BELTED RADIAL

Shoulder

Sidewall

Sipes

CROSS-PLY

Cross-ply casing

Tread groove

Textile belting ply

Radial casing

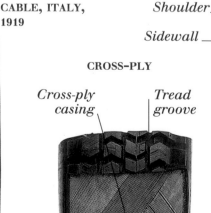

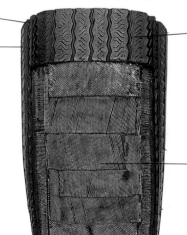

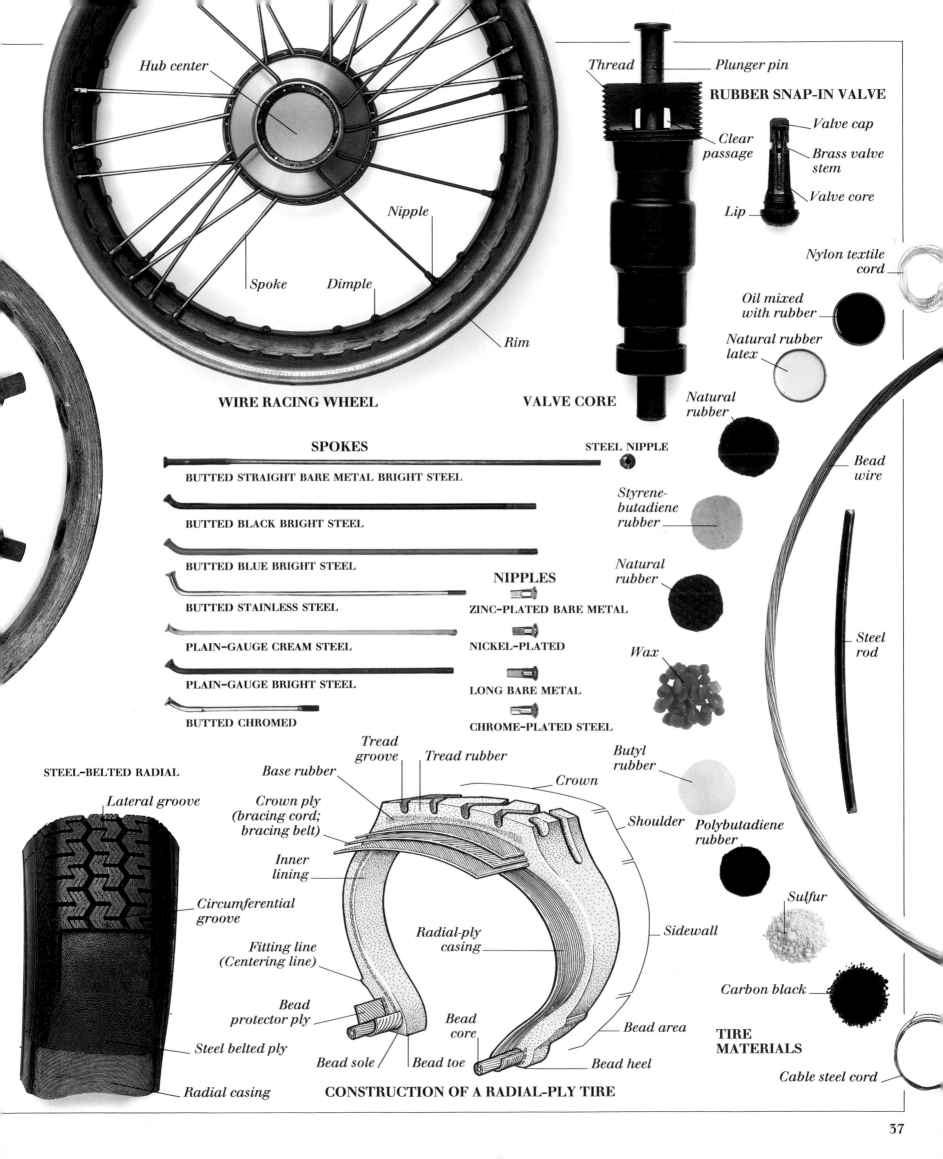

WIRE RACING WHEEL

Hub center

Nipple

Spoke

Dimple

Rim

RUBBER SNAP-IN VALVE

Thread

Plunger pin

Clear passage

Valve cap

Brass valve stem

Valve core

Lip

VALVE CORE

Nylon textile cord

Oil mixed with rubber

Natural rubber latex

Natural rubber

Bead wire

SPOKES

BUTTED STRAIGHT BARE METAL BRIGHT STEEL

BUTTED BLACK BRIGHT STEEL

BUTTED BLUE BRIGHT STEEL

BUTTED STAINLESS STEEL

PLAIN-GAUGE CREAM STEEL

PLAIN-GAUGE BRIGHT STEEL

BUTTED CHROMED

STEEL NIPPLE

Styrene-butadiene rubber

Natural rubber

Wax

Steel rod

NIPPLES

ZINC-PLATED BARE METAL

NICKEL-PLATED

LONG BARE METAL

CHROME-PLATED STEEL

STEEL-BELTED RADIAL

Lateral groove

Circumferential groove

Fitting line (Centering line)

Bead protector ply

Steel belted ply

Radial casing

Tread groove

Tread rubber

Base rubber

Crown ply (bracing cord; bracing belt)

Inner lining

Radial-ply casing

Crown

Shoulder

Sidewall

Bead area

Bead heel

Butyl rubber

Polybutadiene rubber

Sulfur

Carbon black

TIRE MATERIALS

Bead sole

Bead toe

Bead core

CONSTRUCTION OF A RADIAL-PLY TIRE

Cable steel cord

Brakes

BRAKES WERE A WEAK POINT of early cars. They often exerted uneven pressure on the wheels, causing the vehicle to pull to one side. Many early cars had wraparound band brakes, but they performed poorly when wet. Drum brakes (brake shoes that expand internally in a drum) on all four wheels became standard in the 1920s, but when used repeatedly, such brakes "fade" (when heat distorts the drums), leading to temporary loss of braking power. The solution, discovered in the 1950s, was to use disc brakes, in which brake pads press against a heat-conducting metal disc. Now, cars use drum brakes only on the rear wheels and disc brakes on the front or on all four wheels.

MODERN DRUM BRAKE

Anti-rattle pin
Anti-rattle spring
Anti-rattle washer
Pull-off spring
Link
Trailing brake shoe
Leading brake shoe
Lock adjuster nut
Adjuster bar
Adjuster bolt
Brake shoe return-spring

Wheel cylinder
Back plate
Brake drum and hub

SPRAG BRAKE

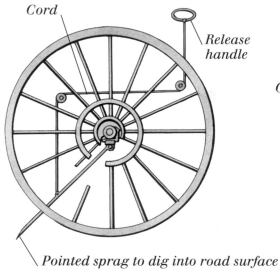

Cord
Release handle
Clevis
Pointed sprag to dig into road surface

RIM BRAKE

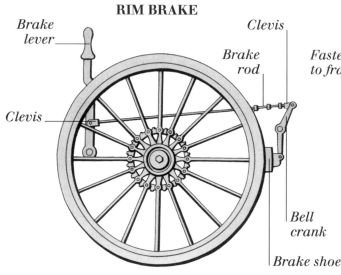

Brake lever
Clevis
Brake rod
Clevis
Bell crank
Brake shoe

WRAPAROUND BAND BRAKE

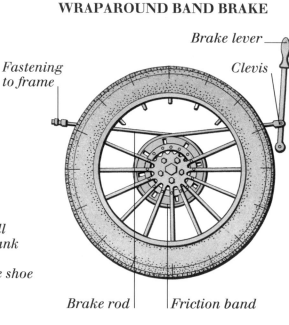

Brake lever
Clevis
Fastening to frame
Brake rod
Friction band

BAND BRAKE

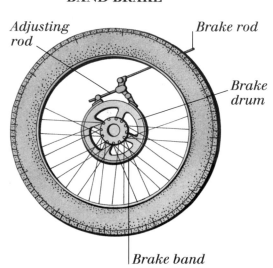

Adjusting rod
Brake rod
Brake drum
Brake band

INTERNAL EXPANDING DRUM BRAKE

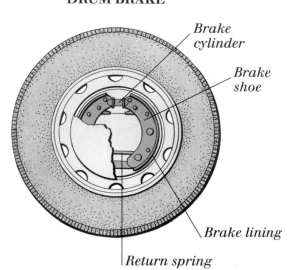

Brake cylinder
Brake shoe
Brake lining
Return spring

DISC BRAKE

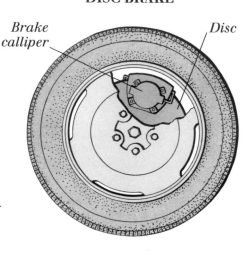

Brake calliper
Disc

MODERN FRONT WHEEL DISC BRAKE

FRONT AND REAR VIEWS OF ANTILOCK BRAKING SYSTEM

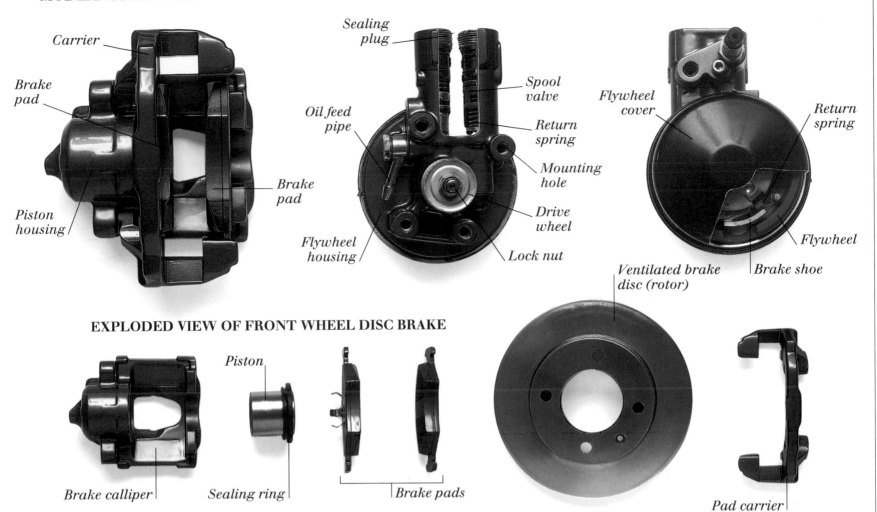

Carrier
Brake pad
Piston housing
Brake pad

Sealing plug
Oil feed pipe
Spool valve
Return spring
Mounting hole
Drive wheel
Flywheel housing
Lock nut

Flywheel cover
Return spring
Flywheel
Ventilated brake disc (rotor)
Brake shoe

EXPLODED VIEW OF FRONT WHEEL DISC BRAKE

Piston
Brake calliper
Sealing ring
Brake pads
Pad carrier

MARKUS MOTOR CARRIAGE WITH WOODEN BLOCK BRAKES, 1887

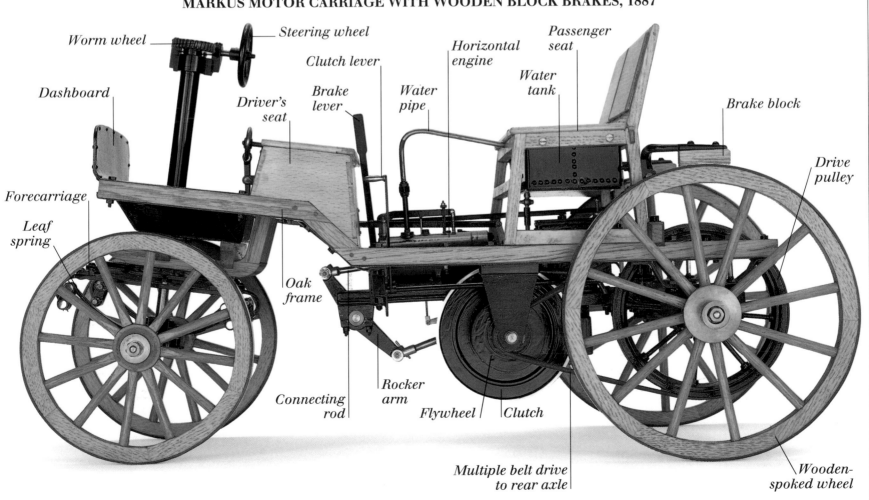

Worm wheel
Steering wheel
Clutch lever
Horizontal engine
Passenger seat
Dashboard
Brake lever
Water pipe
Water tank
Brake block
Driver's seat
Forecarriage
Leaf spring
Oak frame
Drive pulley
Connecting rod
Rocker arm
Flywheel
Clutch
Multiple belt drive to rear axle
Wooden-spoked wheel

Instruments

THE FIRST CARS REQUIRED such frequent attention to fuel, water, and lubricants that no instruments were necessary. The 1904 Mercedes (below) has a "brake-and-gradient meter" for indicating the efficiency of the car, but no speedometer. As the performance of cars improved, speed indicators, like the Cowey and Bowden meters shown here, appeared. The Cowey could also record the speed traveled at points 50 yards apart over the previous 750 yards. Soon, simple fuel and water gauges were added. Modern instrument panels monitor performance using electronic rather than mechanical means. Their readouts are often digital, as shown at right.

MODERN DIGITAL INSTRUMENT PANEL

Fascia air vent
Clock
Battery gauge
Oil gauge
Tachometer (revolution counter)
Stereo control panel
Fan control dial
Heater control
Ventilation control
Fuel-level gauge
Speedometer
Water-temperature gauge

ELECTRIC FUEL GAUGE, c.1930

Bevel gearing
Reduction gear case
Indicator needle
Float arm
Rotating shaft (spindle)
Dashboard gauge
Float
Knurled collar
Flange
Drive cable

COWEY RECORDING SPEED INDICATOR, 1910

Indicator needle
Trip mileage recorder
Brass casing
Casing for worm gearing
Speedometer dial
Indicator needle
Pointer
Speed recording dial
Elapsed speed and distance indicator
Glass cover
Odometer (cyclometer) to record total mileage

NOT TO EXCEED 40 M.P.H
MILES PER HOUR
THE COWEY PATENT RECORDING SPEED INDICATOR
N°B 39
THE COWEY ENGINEERING C°.L°
KEW GARDENS
SW
YARDS BACK
PAST SPEEDS IN MILES PER HOUR

70-HP MERCEDES, 1904

Acetylene headlight
Screw-down greaser (king pin greaser)
Radiator filler cap
Hood rest
Sight-glass oiler (starting oiler)
Front axle
Grab handle
Bail handle
Oil side lamp
Brake-and-gradient meter
Manual oil pump
Engine oil tank
Water pump lubricator

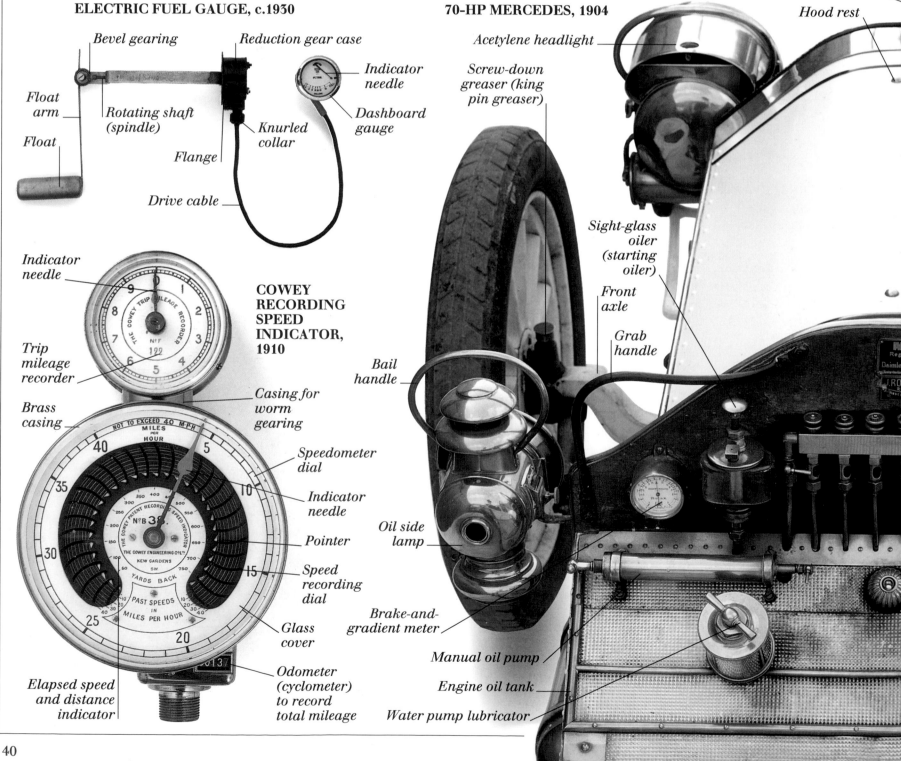

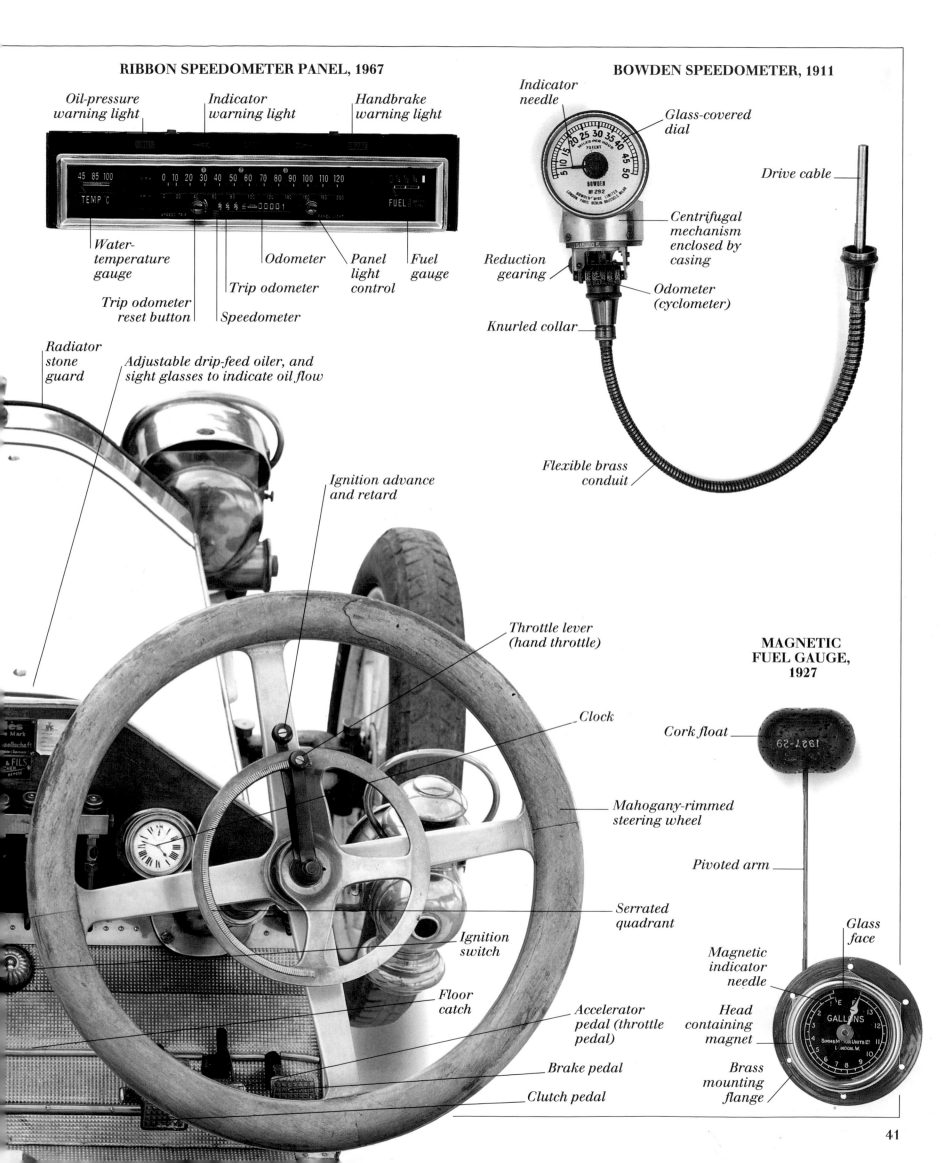

RIBBON SPEEDOMETER PANEL, 1967

Oil-pressure warning light

Indicator warning light

Handbrake warning light

TEMP C

45 85 100

0 10 20 30 40 50 60 70 80 90 100 110 120

00001

FUEL

Water-temperature gauge

Odometer

Panel light control

Fuel gauge

Trip odometer reset button

Trip odometer

Speedometer

BOWDEN SPEEDOMETER, 1911

Indicator needle

Glass-covered dial

Drive cable

Centrifugal mechanism enclosed by casing

Reduction gearing

Odometer (cyclometer)

Knurled collar

Flexible brass conduit

Radiator stone guard

Adjustable drip-feed oiler, and sight glasses to indicate oil flow

Ignition advance and retard

Throttle lever (hand throttle)

Clock

MAGNETIC FUEL GAUGE, 1927

Cork float

Mahogany-rimmed steering wheel

Pivoted arm

Glass face

Serrated quadrant

Magnetic indicator needle

Ignition switch

Head containing magnet

Floor catch

Accelerator pedal (throttle pedal)

Brake pedal

Clutch pedal

Brass mounting flange

Electrical systems

THE FIRST USE OF ELECTRICITY in cars was small batteries used to power the ignition system. The first electric headlamps appeared in 1905 and gradually replaced those using acetylene gas. Electricity is used extensively in modern cars. Lighting, ignition, locking, windows, stereo systems, instruments, and alarms are all controlled electrically, and are linked to the power source by a complex wiring harness (loom). Today, electrical systems often incorporate computers, which may control various functions, even including adjusting the position of the driver's seat to suit the needs of individual drivers.

MERCEDES COMPUTERIZED ELECTRIC SEAT

Drive belt

Gearbox and backrest adjustment motor

Back release

Backrest release

Seat belt

Drive cable

Head restraint motor

Back-lock motor

Runner

Gearbox

Fire extinguisher mounting bracket

Front seat lift

Main control harness

Lid for carbide chamber

Retaining nut

Carbide chamber

Water chamber

DRIP-FEED ACETYLENE GENERATOR, 1911

WIRING HARNESS OF A MODERN CAR

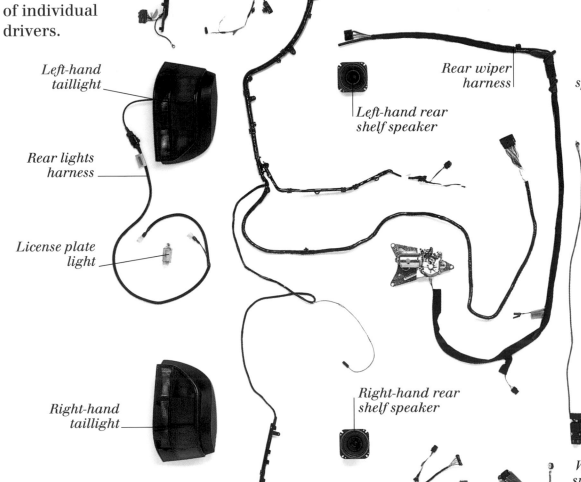

Left-hand taillight

Rear lights harness

License plate light

Right-hand taillight

Rear windshield heater and trunk light harness

Rear wiper harness

Left-hand rear shelf speaker

Right-hand rear shelf speaker

Radio antenna

Door radio speaker

Fuse board assembly

Fuse box

Lighting switch

Dash harness

Instrument panel assembly

Wiper switch

Right-hand side harness

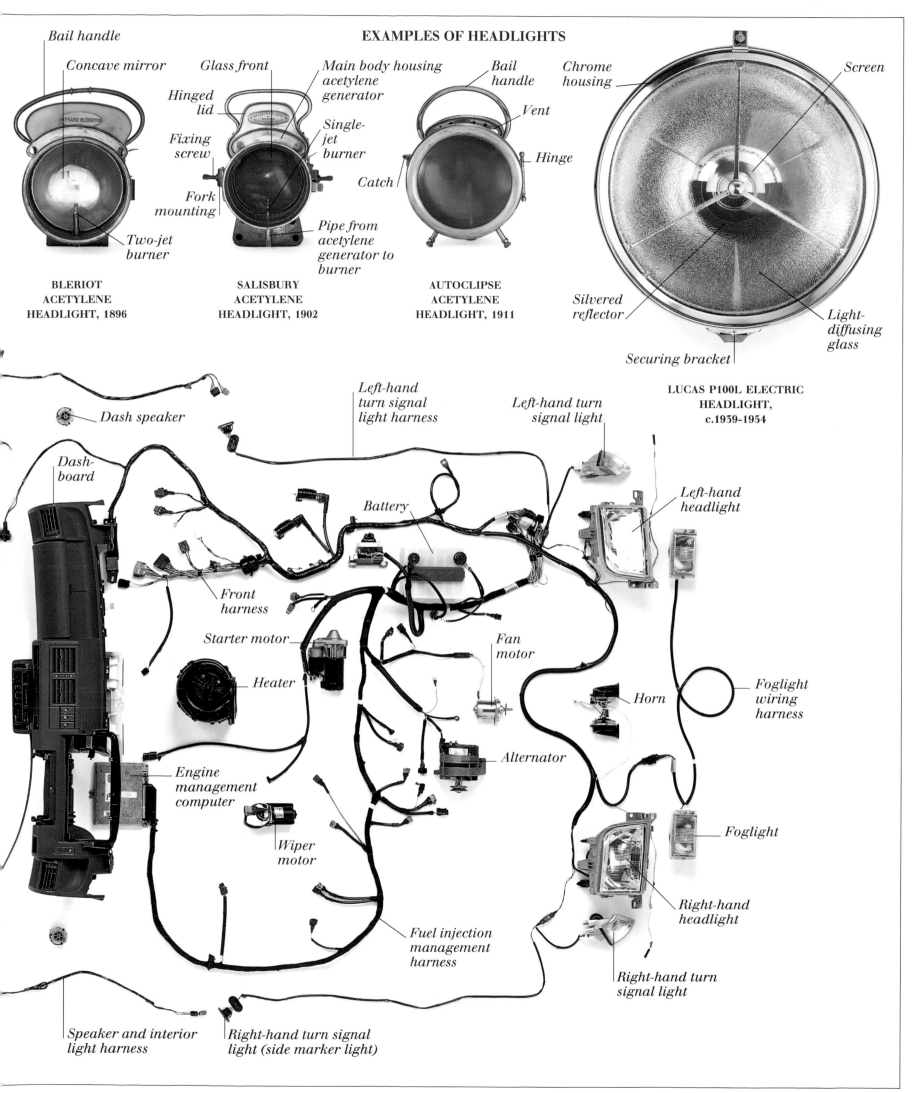

EXAMPLES OF HEADLIGHTS

Bail handle

Concave mirror

Two-jet burner

BLERIOT ACETYLENE HEADLIGHT, 1896

Glass front

Hinged lid

Fixing screw

Fork mounting

Main body housing acetylene generator

Single-jet burner

Pipe from acetylene generator to burner

SALISBURY ACETYLENE HEADLIGHT, 1902

Bail handle

Vent

Catch

Hinge

AUTOCLIPSE ACETYLENE HEADLIGHT, 1911

Chrome housing

Screen

Silvered reflector

Securing bracket

Light-diffusing glass

LUCAS P100L ELECTRIC HEADLIGHT, c.1939-1954

Dash speaker

Dashboard

Front harness

Starter motor

Heater

Engine management computer

Wiper motor

Left-hand turn signal light harness

Battery

Fan motor

Alternator

Fuel injection management harness

Left-hand turn signal light

Left-hand headlight

Horn

Foglight wiring harness

Foglight

Right-hand headlight

Right-hand turn signal light

Speaker and interior light harness

Right-hand turn signal light (side marker light)

Modern bodywork

THE BODY OF A MODERN MASS–PRODUCED CAR is built on the monocoque (single-shell) principle, in which the roof, side panels, and floor are welded into a single integral unit. This bodyshell protects and supports the car's internal parts. Steel and glass are used to construct the bodyshell, creating a unit that is both light and strong. Its lightness helps to conserve energy, while its strength protects the occupants. Modern bodywork is designed with the aid of computers, which are used to predict factors such as aerodynamic efficiency and impact resistance. High technology is also employed on the production line, where robots are used to assemble, weld, and paint the body.

RENAULT
LOGO

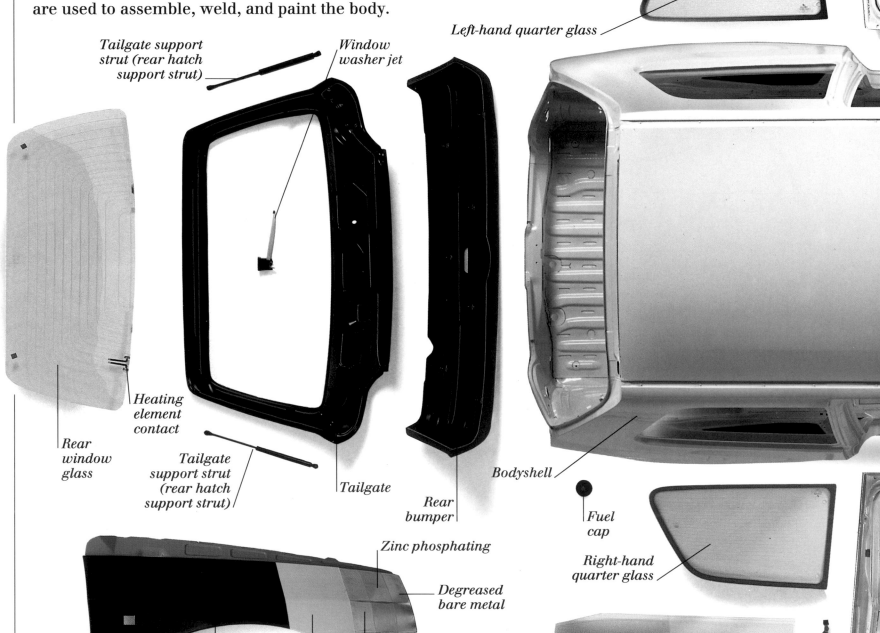

Door handle

Door lock

Left-hand door glass

Left-hand quarter glass

Tailgate support strut (rear hatch support strut)

Window washer jet

Heating element contact

Rear window glass

Tailgate support strut (rear hatch support strut)

Tailgate

Rear bumper

Bodyshell

Fuel cap

Zinc phosphating

Degreased bare metal

Right-hand quarter glass

Primer

Base coat color

Cataphoresic coating

Right-hand door glass

Door key and lock

Clear coat

Chrome passivation

Door handle

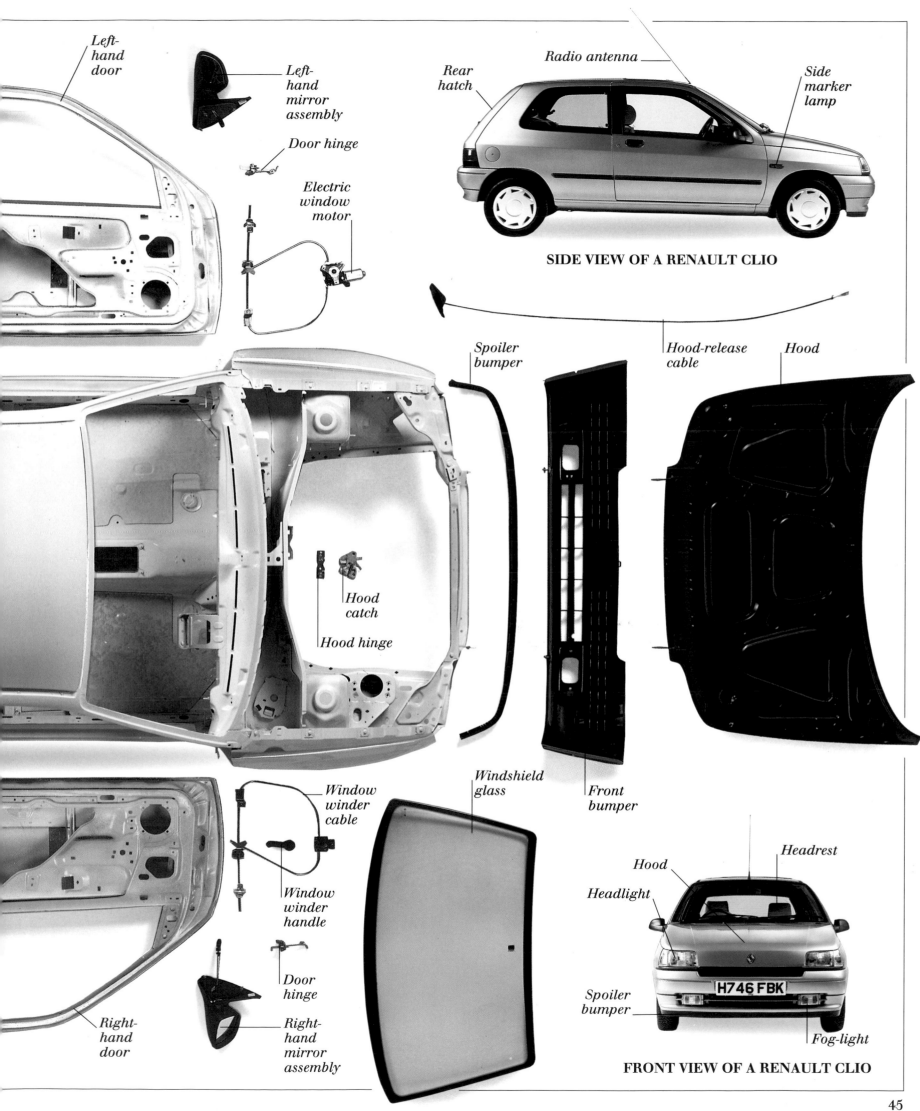

Left-hand door

Left-hand mirror assembly

Door hinge

Electric window motor

Radio antenna

Rear hatch

Side marker lamp

SIDE VIEW OF A RENAULT CLIO

Spoiler bumper

Hood-release cable

Hood

Hood catch

Hood hinge

Window winder cable

Window winder handle

Door hinge

Right-hand door

Right-hand mirror assembly

Windshield glass

Front bumper

Hood

Headrest

Headlight

Spoiler bumper

Fog-light

H746 FBK

FRONT VIEW OF A RENAULT CLIO

Modern components

A TYPICAL MODERN CAR has several thousand individual mechanical components. These are assembled to form the car's various mechanical systems: engine and exhaust, transmission, steering, suspension, and brakes. To ensure that each system functions properly, components are manufactured to extremely fine tolerances—to within about one ten-thousandth of an inch in some cases.

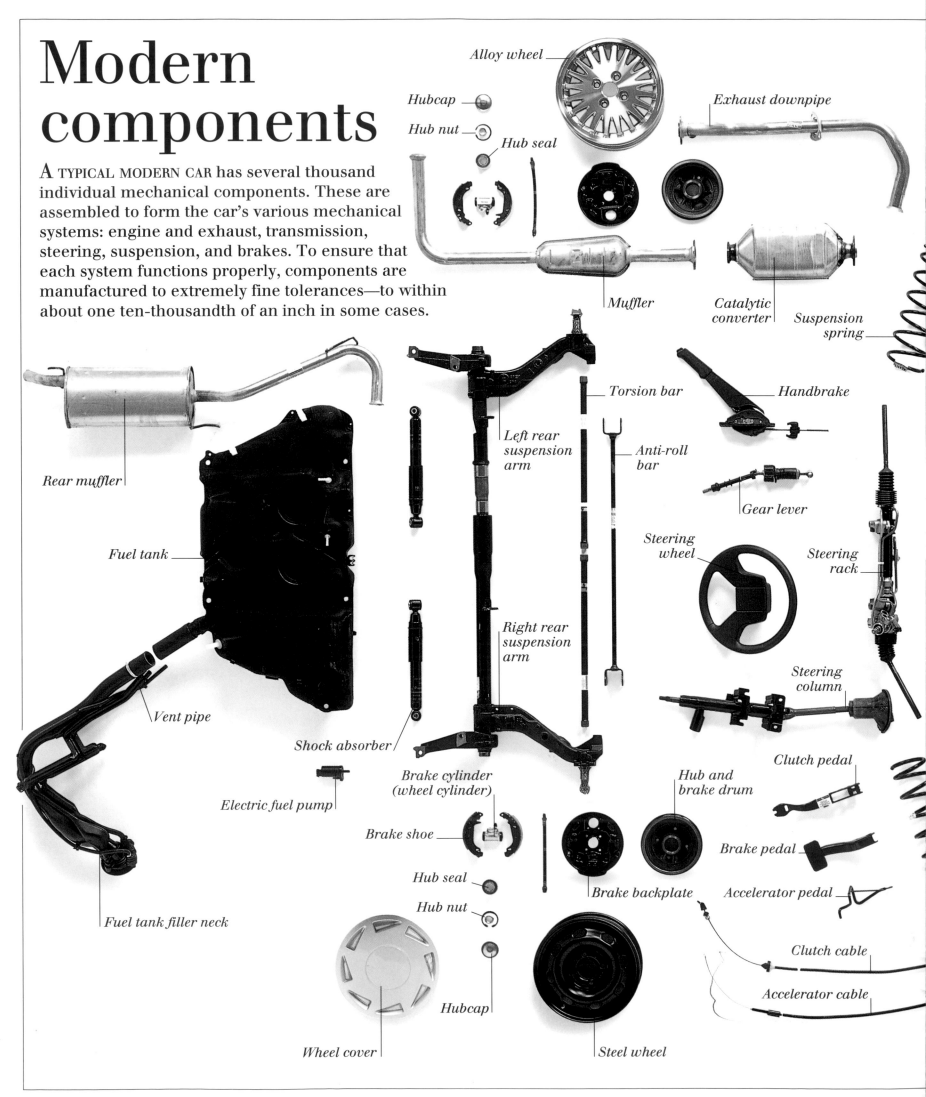

Alloy wheel

Hubcap

Hub nut

Hub seal

Exhaust downpipe

Muffler

Catalytic converter

Suspension spring

Rear muffler

Torsion bar

Handbrake

Left rear suspension arm

Anti-roll bar

Gear lever

Fuel tank

Steering wheel

Steering rack

Right rear suspension arm

Steering column

Clutch pedal

Hub and brake drum

Vent pipe

Shock absorber

Brake cylinder (wheel cylinder)

Electric fuel pump

Brake pedal

Brake shoe

Accelerator pedal

Hub seal

Brake backplate

Fuel tank filler neck

Hub nut

Clutch cable

Accelerator cable

Hubcap

Wheel cover

Steel wheel

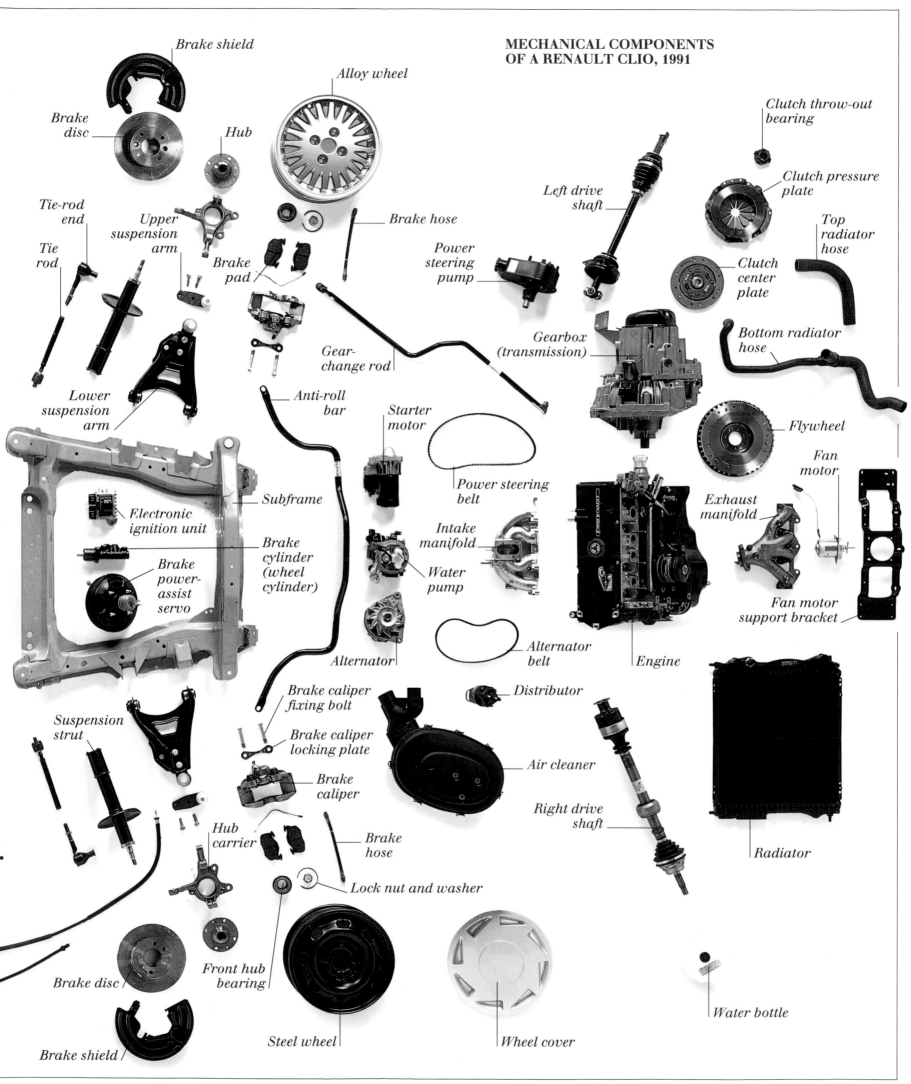

Brake shield

Alloy wheel

Brake disc

Hub

Clutch throw-out bearing

Brake hose

Left drive shaft

Clutch pressure plate

Tie-rod end

Upper suspension arm

Brake pad

Power steering pump

Clutch center plate

Top radiator hose

Tie rod

Gear-change rod

Gearbox (transmission)

Bottom radiator hose

Lower suspension arm

Anti-roll bar

Starter motor

Flywheel

Fan motor

Subframe

Power steering belt

Exhaust manifold

Electronic ignition unit

Intake manifold

Brake cylinder (wheel cylinder)

Brake power-assist servo

Water pump

Fan motor support bracket

Alternator belt

Alternator

Engine

Brake caliper fixing bolt

Distributor

Suspension strut

Brake caliper locking plate

Air cleaner

Brake caliper

Right drive shaft

Hub carrier

Brake hose

Radiator

Lock nut and washer

Front hub bearing

Brake disc

Steel wheel

Wheel cover

Water bottle

Brake shield

47

Modern trim

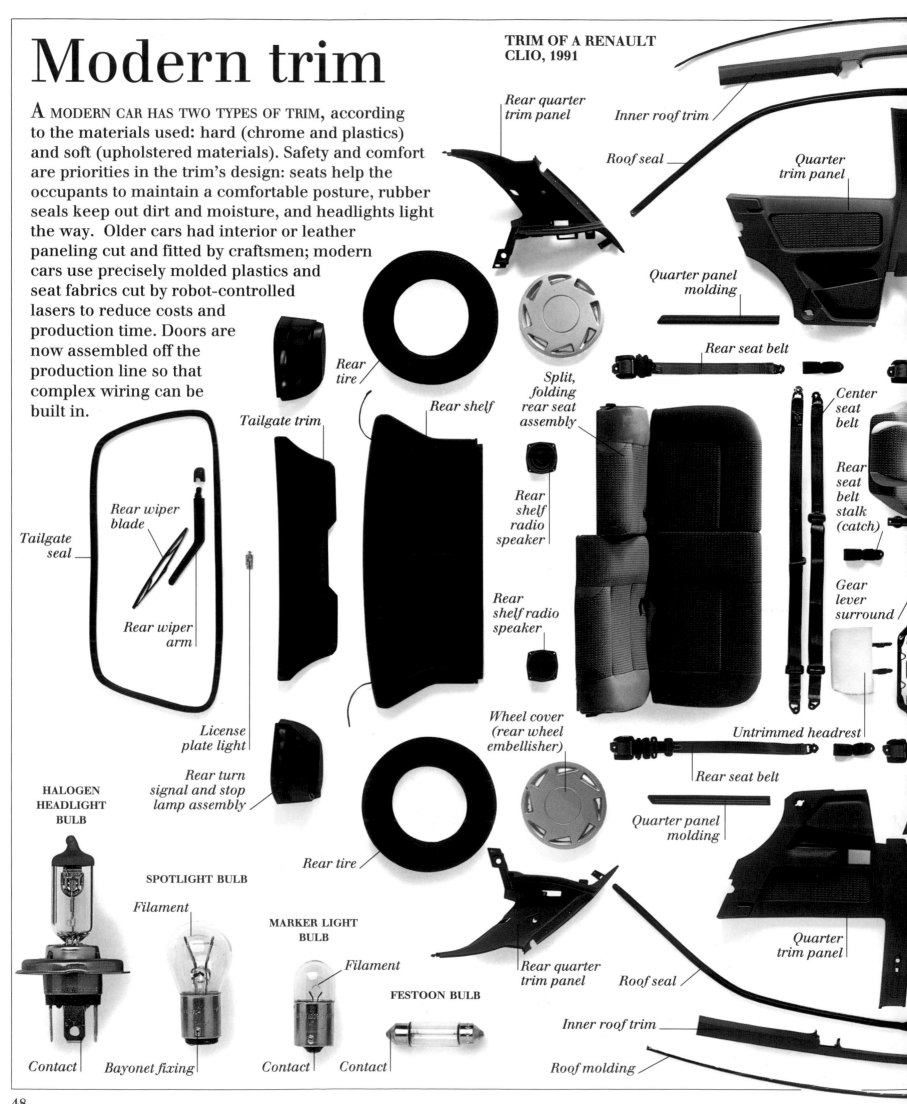

A MODERN CAR HAS TWO TYPES OF TRIM, according to the materials used: hard (chrome and plastics) and soft (upholstered materials). Safety and comfort are priorities in the trim's design: seats help the occupants to maintain a comfortable posture, rubber seals keep out dirt and moisture, and headlights light the way. Older cars had interior or leather paneling cut and fitted by craftsmen; modern cars use precisely molded plastics and seat fabrics cut by robot-controlled lasers to reduce costs and production time. Doors are now assembled off the production line so that complex wiring can be built in.

TRIM OF A RENAULT CLIO, 1991

Rear quarter trim panel

Inner roof trim

Roof seal

Quarter trim panel

Quarter panel molding

Rear seat belt

Center seat belt

Rear tire

Split, folding rear seat assembly

Rear seat belt stalk (catch)

Tailgate trim

Rear shelf

Rear shelf radio speaker

Rear shelf radio speaker

Gear lever surround

Tailgate seal

Rear wiper blade

Rear wiper arm

License plate light

Rear turn signal and stop lamp assembly

Wheel cover (rear wheel embellisher)

Untrimmed headrest

Rear seat belt

Quarter panel molding

HALOGEN HEADLIGHT BULB

SPOTLIGHT BULB

Filament

Rear tire

Quarter trim panel

MARKER LIGHT BULB

Filament

Rear quarter trim panel

Roof seal

FESTOON BULB

Inner roof trim

Contact

Bayonet fixing

Contact

Contact

Roof molding

48

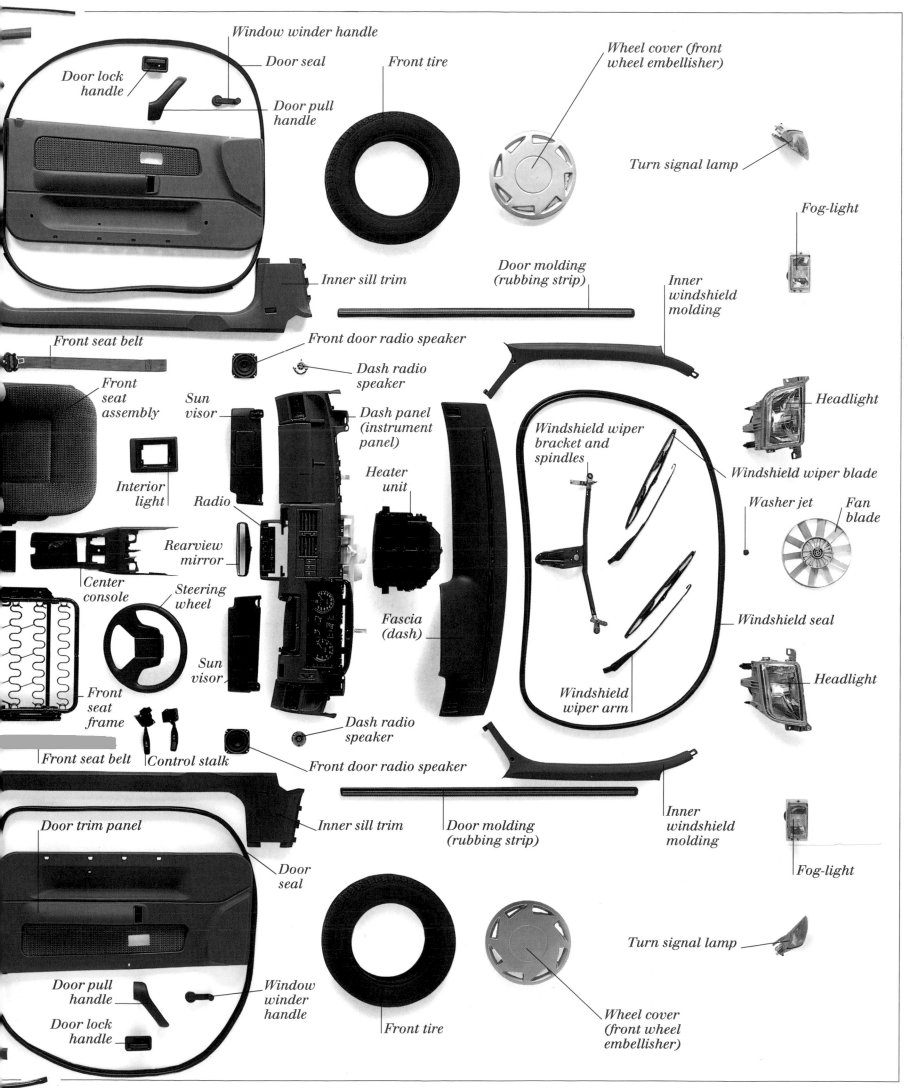

Window winder handle

Door seal

Front tire

Wheel cover (front wheel embellisher)

Door lock handle

Door pull handle

Turn signal lamp

Fog-light

Inner sill trim

Door molding (rubbing strip)

Inner windshield molding

Front seat belt

Front door radio speaker

Dash radio speaker

Front seat assembly

Sun visor

Dash panel (instrument panel)

Windshield wiper bracket and spindles

Headlight

Interior light

Radio

Heater unit

Windshield wiper blade

Washer jet

Fan blade

Rearview mirror

Center console

Steering wheel

Fascia (dash)

Windshield seal

Sun visor

Headlight

Front seat frame

Windshield wiper arm

Front seat belt

Control stalk

Dash radio speaker

Front door radio speaker

Inner windshield molding

Door trim panel

Inner sill trim

Door molding (rubbing strip)

Fog-light

Door seal

Door pull handle

Window winder handle

Turn signal lamp

Door lock handle

Front tire

Wheel cover (front wheel embellisher)

49

Coachbuilt cars

IN THE EARLY DAYS OF MOTORING, the purchasers of high-quality cars bought a chassis and then had a body built to their individual requirements by a master coachbuilder. Two examples are the Rolls-Royces on these pages. Early car bodies were built along principles similar to those used in horse-drawn carriage construction, although allowances had to be made for the extra stresses that made one year's use of a car equivalent to several of a horse-drawn carriage. For this reason, the wings, running boards, and wooden framework (which was covered by hand-formed wooden or metal paneling) were strengthened by iron stays made by blacksmiths. The bodywork was then finished with many coats of hand-applied paint and varnish.

ASH FRAME

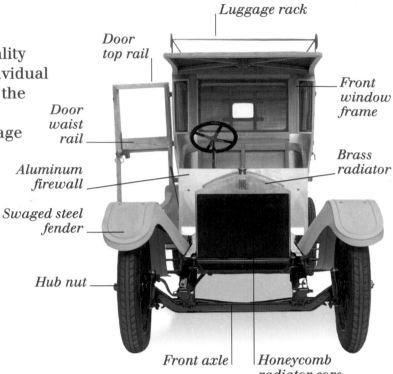

FRONT VIEW OF "D" FRONT LIMOUSINE

Luggage rack

Door top rail

Front window frame

Door waist rail

Brass radiator

Aluminum firewall

Swaged steel fender

Hub nut

Front axle

Honeycomb radiator core

1911 ROLLS-ROYCE SILVER GHOST "D" FRONT LIMOUSINE

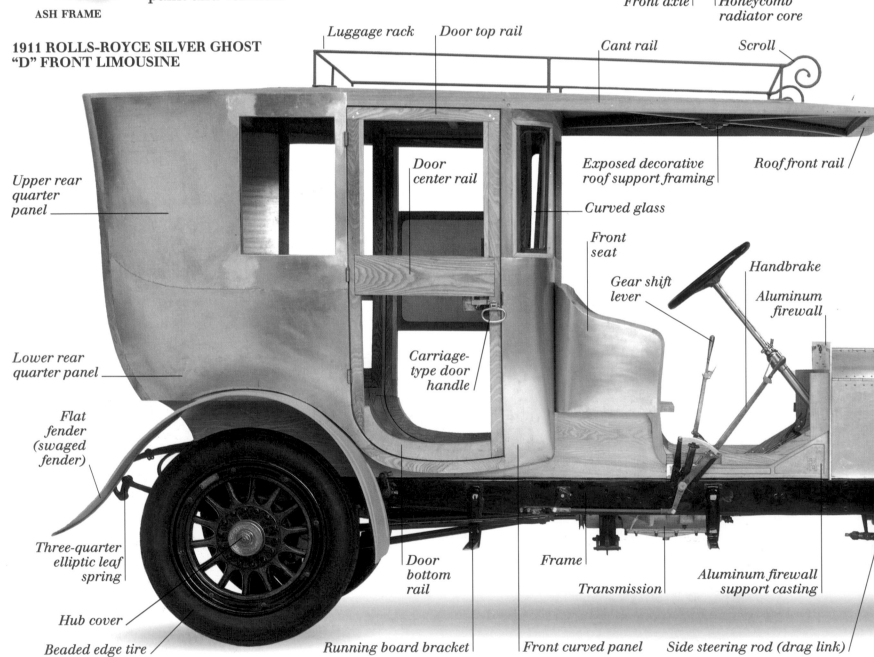

Luggage rack

Door top rail

Cant rail

Scroll

Door center rail

Exposed decorative roof support framing

Roof front rail

Upper rear quarter panel

Curved glass

Front seat

Handbrake

Gear shift lever

Aluminum firewall

Lower rear quarter panel

Carriage-type door handle

Flat fender (swaged fender)

Three-quarter elliptic leaf spring

Door bottom rail

Frame

Aluminum firewall support casting

Hub cover

Transmission

Beaded edge tire

Running board bracket

Front curved panel

Side steering rod (drag link)

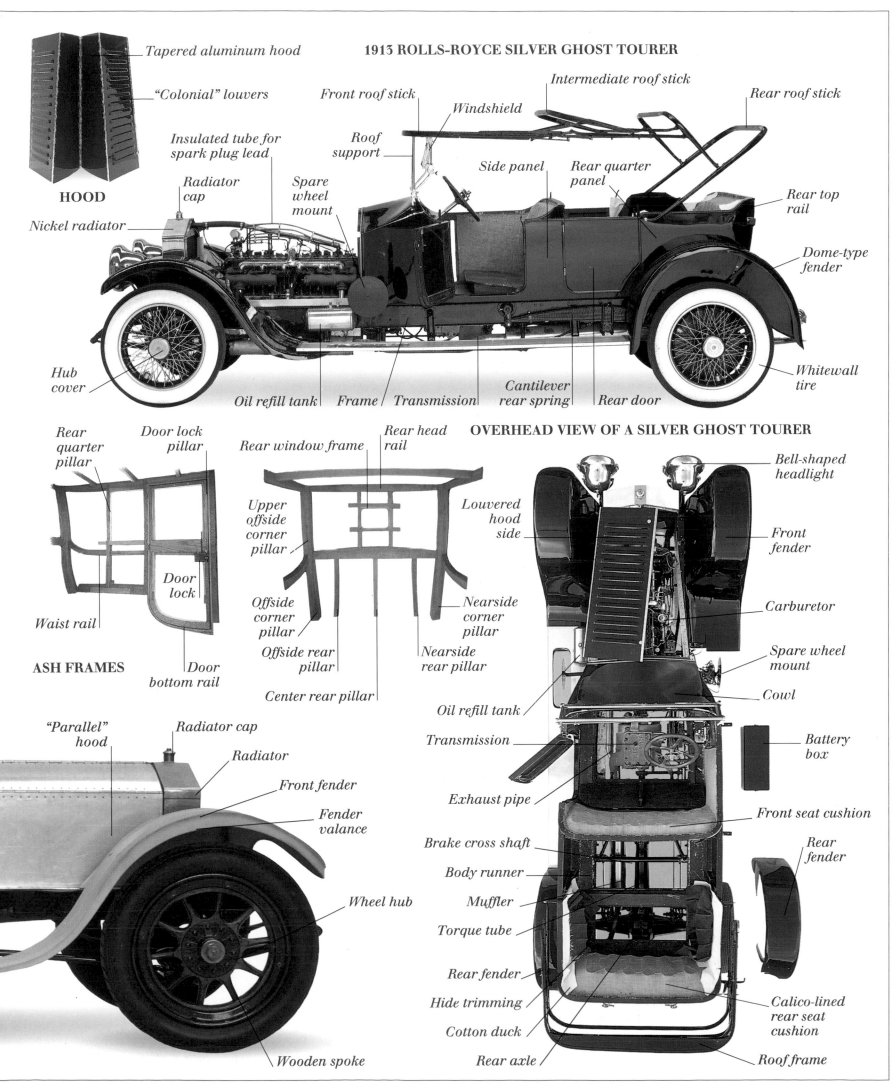

HOOD

Tapered aluminum hood

"Colonial" louvers

1913 ROLLS-ROYCE SILVER GHOST TOURER

Front roof stick

Windshield

Intermediate roof stick

Rear roof stick

Insulated tube for spark plug lead

Roof support

Side panel

Rear quarter panel

Rear top rail

Radiator cap

Spare wheel mount

Nickel radiator

Dome-type fender

Hub cover

Whitewall tire

Oil refill tank Frame Transmission

Cantilever rear spring

Rear door

Rear quarter pillar

Door lock pillar

Rear window frame

Rear head rail

OVERHEAD VIEW OF A SILVER GHOST TOURER

Bell-shaped headlight

Upper offside corner pillar

Louvered hood side

Front fender

Door lock

Carburetor

Offside corner pillar

Nearside corner pillar

Spare wheel mount

Waist rail

ASH FRAMES

Door bottom rail

Offside rear pillar

Nearside rear pillar

Cowl

Center rear pillar

Oil refill tank

Battery box

Transmission

"Parallel" hood

Radiator cap

Radiator

Exhaust pipe

Front seat cushion

Front fender

Fender valance

Brake cross shaft

Rear fender

Body runner

Wheel hub

Muffler

Torque tube

Rear fender

Hide trimming

Calico-lined rear seat cushion

Cotton duck

Wooden spoke

Rear axle

Roof frame

Cars assembled by hand

LATER COACHBUILT CARS, such as the 1932 Alvis shown here, combined traditional craftsmanship with elements of mass-production. Their bodies could be assembled by hand in large numbers by using standardized wooden components and mechanically pressed exterior metal panelwork. Where individually built bodies used timber cut to shape by craftsmen, other coachbuilt bodies were made using template-cut timber, which could be produced in greater quantities. Such developments enabled the costs of coachwork to be kept down. By the end of the 1930s, all-steel bodies had become virtually universal, and, by the end of the 1950s, the economic advantages of mass-production meant that the craft of coachbuilding became limited to the restoration of vintage vehicles and the production of exclusive cars.

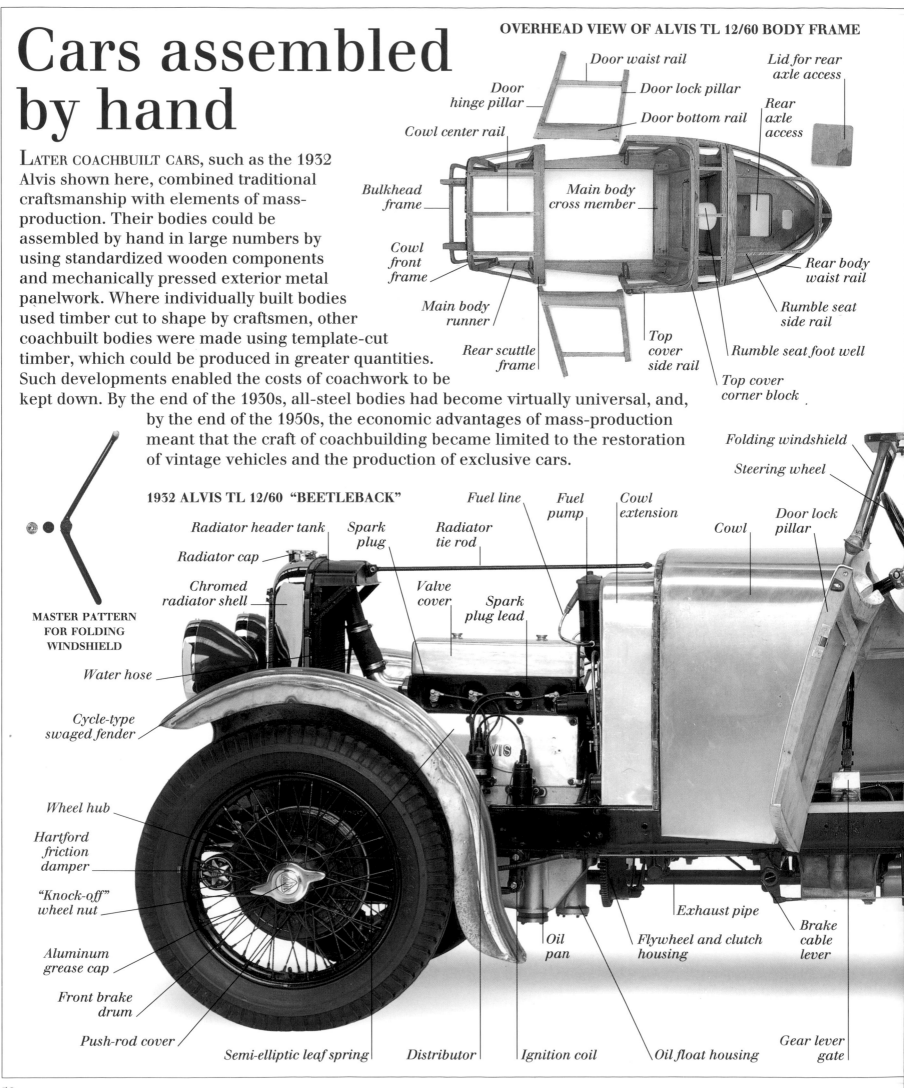

OVERHEAD VIEW OF ALVIS TL 12/60 BODY FRAME

Door waist rail
Door hinge pillar
Door lock pillar
Lid for rear axle access
Door bottom rail
Rear axle access
Cowl center rail
Bulkhead frame
Main body cross member
Cowl front frame
Rear body waist rail
Main body runner
Rumble seat side rail
Rear scuttle frame
Top cover side rail
Rumble seat foot well
Top cover corner block

MASTER PATTERN FOR FOLDING WINDSHIELD

1932 ALVIS TL 12/60 "BEETLEBACK"

Radiator header tank
Radiator cap
Spark plug
Fuel line
Fuel pump
Cowl extension
Folding windshield
Steering wheel
Cowl
Door lock pillar
Chromed radiator shell
Radiator tie rod
Valve cover
Spark plug lead
Water hose
Cycle-type swaged fender
Wheel hub
Hartford friction damper
"Knock-off" wheel nut
Aluminum grease cap
Front brake drum
Exhaust pipe
Brake cable lever
Oil pan
Flywheel and clutch housing
Push-rod cover
Semi-elliptic leaf spring
Distributor
Ignition coil
Oil float housing
Gear lever gate

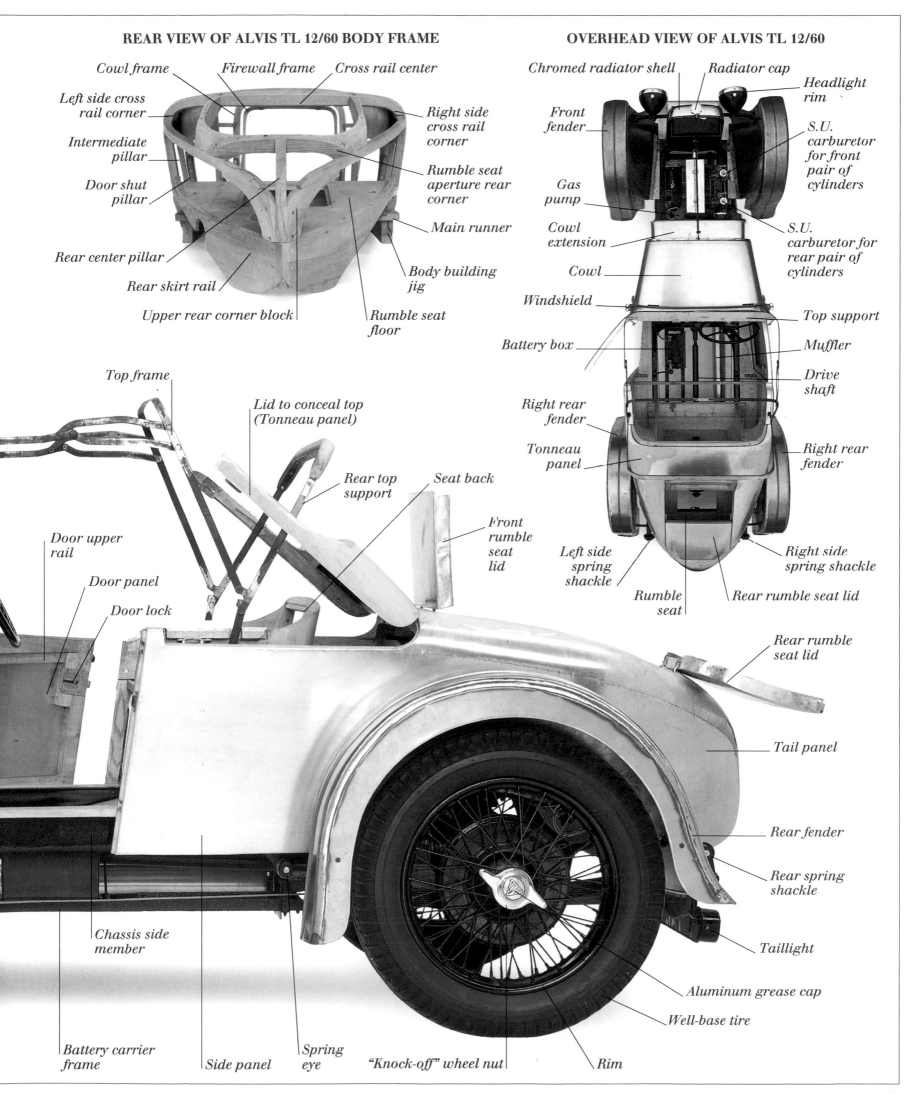

REAR VIEW OF ALVIS TL 12/60 BODY FRAME

Cowl frame
Firewall frame
Cross rail center
Left side cross rail corner
Right side cross rail corner
Intermediate pillar
Rumble seat aperture rear corner
Door shut pillar
Main runner
Rear center pillar
Body building jig
Rear skirt rail
Upper rear corner block
Rumble seat floor

OVERHEAD VIEW OF ALVIS TL 12/60

Chromed radiator shell
Radiator cap
Headlight rim
Front fender
S.U. carburetor for front pair of cylinders
Gas pump
S.U. carburetor for rear pair of cylinders
Cowl extension
Cowl
Top support
Windshield
Battery box
Muffler
Drive shaft
Right rear fender
Right rear fender
Tonneau panel
Left side spring shackle
Right side spring shackle
Rumble seat
Rear rumble seat lid

Top frame
Lid to conceal top (Tonneau panel)
Rear top support
Seat back
Front rumble seat lid
Door upper rail
Door panel
Door lock
Rear rumble seat lid
Tail panel
Rear fender
Rear spring shackle
Chassis side member
Taillight
Battery carrier frame
Side panel
Spring eye
"Knock-off" wheel nut
Rim
Aluminum grease cap
Well-base tire

53

Trim and upholstery

"TRIM" REFERS TO the embellishments of a car, such as the seats, windows, tires, and decoration. "Upholstery" refers to the soft materials used. Cars reached a peak of ostentation with the American models of the 1950s, like the Cadillac Eldorado. Such cars often had large amounts of chrome-plated metalwork and extravagantly upholstered interiors; some even had gold-plated "brightwork" (polished metalwork). Although seats originally used horsehair and individually pocketed springs, they are now usually made with foam filling, which can be molded to the required shape. Many luxury cars still use hand-stitched leather hides for their upholstery and matched wood veneers to trim their dashboards and door cappings.

FRONT VIEW OF CADILLAC ELDORADO, 1954

Radio antenna

Hood crest

Hood ornament

Rearview mirror

Windshield

Steering wheel

Hood

Spotlight and door mirror

Front fender

Headlight unit

Headlight surround

Chrome molding

Turn signal housing

Turn signal

Cross-ply whitewall tire

Overrider support

Grille upright

Bumper

Grille center bar

Overrider (Dagmar)

Vee motif

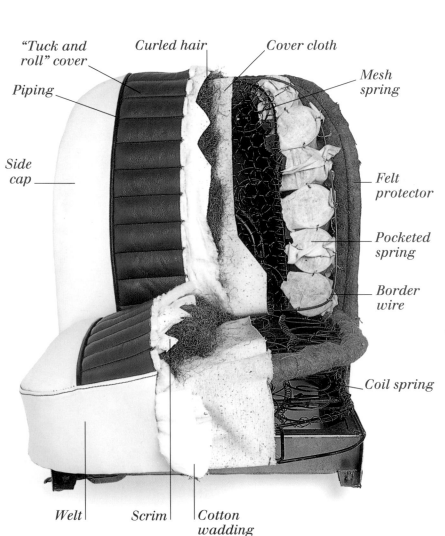

"Tuck and roll" cover

Curled hair

Cover cloth

Piping

Mesh spring

Side cap

Felt protector

Pocketed spring

Border wire

Coil spring

Welt

Scrim

Cotton wadding

SECTIONED TRADITIONAL SPRUNG SEAT

Headrest

Headrest insert panel

Back

Tubular frame

Wire framing

Support spring

Seat rake adjuster (seat angle adjuster)

Seat slide mounting bracket

Base frame

Foam flute pad

Front cushion pan

Foam cushion

Rubber diaphragm

SECTIONED MODERN SEAT

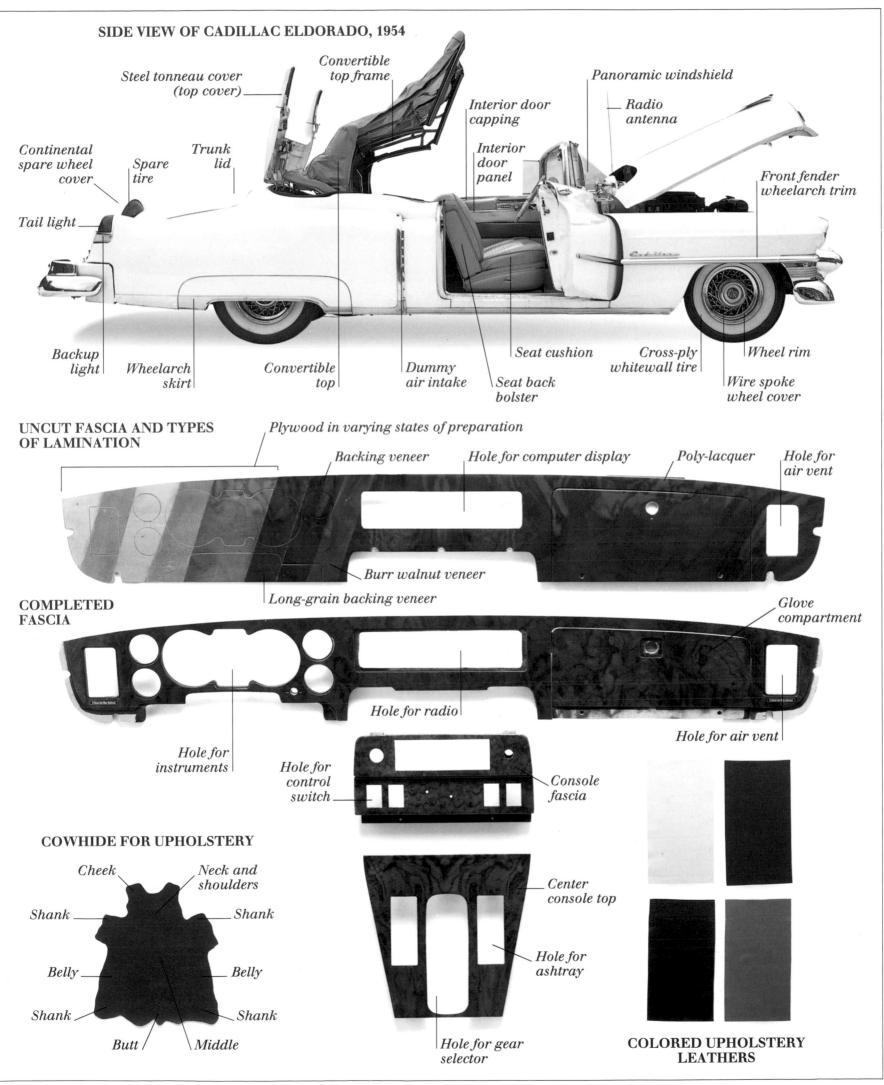

SIDE VIEW OF CADILLAC ELDORADO, 1954

Steel tonneau cover (top cover)

Convertible top frame

Interior door capping

Panoramic windshield

Radio antenna

Continental spare wheel cover

Spare tire

Trunk lid

Interior door panel

Front fender wheelarch trim

Tail light

Backup light

Wheelarch skirt

Convertible top

Dummy air intake

Seat back bolster

Seat cushion

Cross-ply whitewall tire

Wheel rim

Wire spoke wheel cover

UNCUT FASCIA AND TYPES OF LAMINATION

Plywood in varying states of preparation

Backing veneer

Hole for computer display

Poly-lacquer

Hole for air vent

Burr walnut veneer

Long-grain backing veneer

COMPLETED FASCIA

Glove compartment

Hole for instruments

Hole for radio

Hole for air vent

Hole for control switch

Console fascia

COWHIDE FOR UPHOLSTERY

Cheek

Neck and shoulders

Shank

Shank

Belly

Belly

Shank

Shank

Butt

Middle

Center console top

Hole for ashtray

Hole for gear selector

COLORED UPHOLSTERY LEATHERS

All-terrain vehicles

THE MODERN ALL-TERRAIN VEHICLE has its origins in the American military Jeep of the 1940s and the British Land Rover. Such vehicles have been used for a wide range of purposes, from safari travel to fire fighting. The principal special features of such cars—including four- or six-wheel drive, high ground clearance, and toughened braking, suspension, and transmission systems—are designed to enable driving under the most difficult off-road conditions. The vehicle shown here is equipped for safari travel and carries a comprehensive range of survival gear.

COOKING EQUIPMENT

TWO-BURNER ALCOHOL STOVE

Handle for all pans

Flame regulator

Wick

Cooking pot

Zipper

Mosquito netting

Ventilation flap

Tie

Locking fuel filler cap

Dust filter

Raised air intake

Guard

HAND WINCH

SIDE VIEW OF PINZGAUER TURBO D

Folding rooftop tent

Galvanized roof-rack

Steel body

Jerrycan

Spare wheel and tire

Bodyside molding (rub strip)

TIRE PUMP

Pressure gauge

TIRE IRON

Heavy-duty shovel

Tubular backbone chassis

Fuel tank

Metal jerrycan for fuel

Plastic jerrycan for water

LEFT-HAND
TREAD PLATE

RIGHT-HAND
TREAD PLATE

TOW STRAP

HEAVY-DUTY
SHACKLE

SAFETY WINDSHIELD CLAMPS

WASHING BUCKET

Radio aerial

Observation
roof hatch

Grab
handle

Rearview
mirror

Windshield
washer
bottle

Wrap-
around
bumper

Access step

SECURITY
CHAIN

FRONT VIEW OF PINZGAUER TURBO D

Observation
roof hatch

Radio aerial

Galvanized
roof-rack

Laminated
windshield

Rearview
mirror

Air vent

Indicator

Radiator
grille

Headlight
guard

Headlight

External
step

Independent
swing axle

Locking
differential

Towing
loop

All-terrain
tire

REAR VIEW OF PINZGAUER TURBO D

Roof-rack

Observation
platform

External
step for roof

Jerrycan

Spare
wheel

Jerrycan
carrier

Bodyside
molding (rub
strip)

Offset door
hinge

Rear
bumper

Rear light
cluster

Door and
wheel
support
frame

Mudflap

Off-road
tire

Locking
differential

Independent swing axle

Racing cars

SINCE MOTORING BEGAN, racing cars have been a major focus of innovation in car design. Features that are now commonplace, such as disc brakes, turbochargers, and even safety belts, were used first on competition cars. Research into racing cars has contributed to a new understanding of engine performance, aerodynamics, and tire adhesion, and has led to the development of ultra-light materials such as carbon-fiber for car bodies. Like the 1937 Bugatti Type 57S below, today's Williams Formula One car has a low, streamlined body and an open cockpit. Unlike its forerunner, it also has a front wing that pushes the front wheels firmly on to the track, huge slick tires for extra grip, and electrical sensors that continually relay information to the pits about the car's performance.

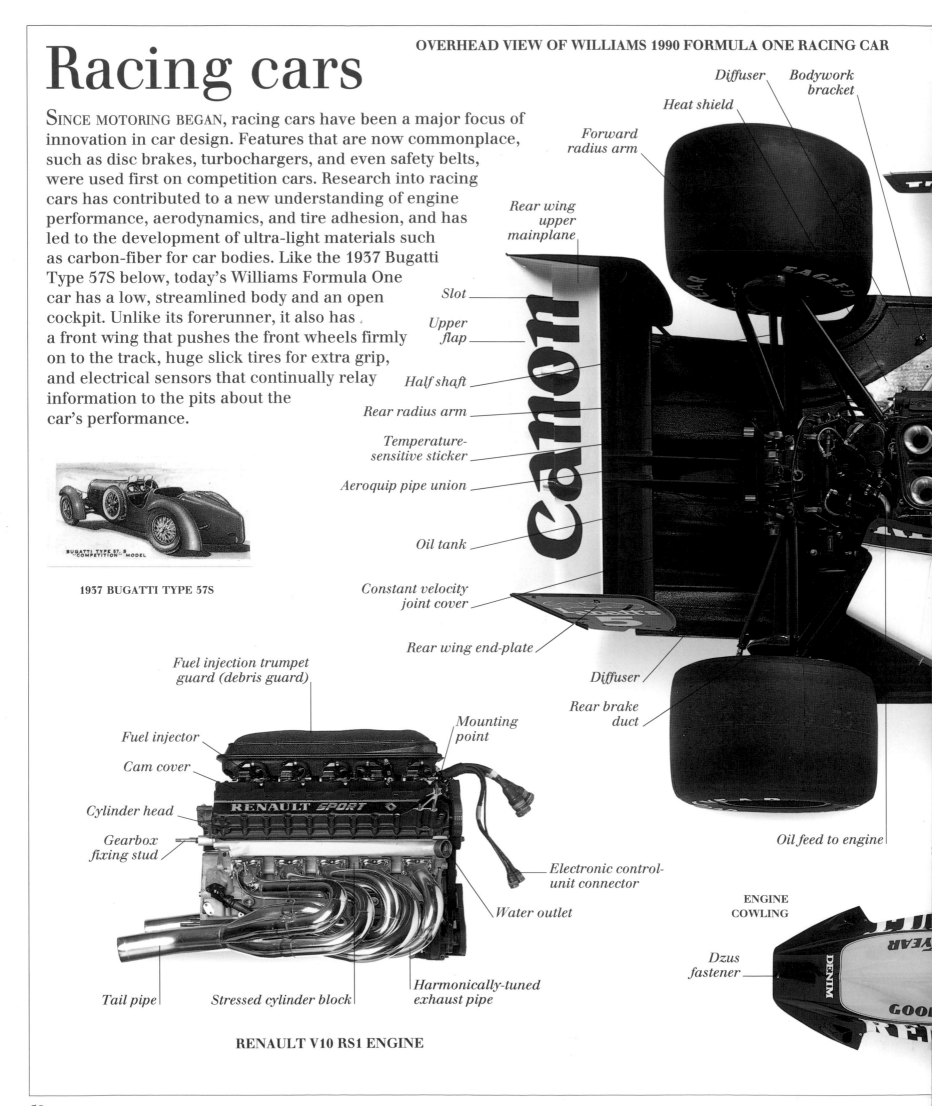

1937 BUGATTI TYPE 57S

Diffuser

Bodywork bracket

Heat shield

Forward radius arm

Rear wing upper mainplane

Slot

Upper flap

Half shaft

Rear radius arm

Temperature-sensitive sticker

Aeroquip pipe union

Oil tank

Constant velocity joint cover

Rear wing end-plate

Diffuser

Rear brake duct

Oil feed to engine

ENGINE COWLING

Dzus fastener

Fuel injection trumpet guard (debris guard)

Fuel injector

Cam cover

Cylinder head

Gearbox fixing stud

Mounting point

Electronic control-unit connector

Water outlet

Tail pipe

Stressed cylinder block

Harmonically-tuned exhaust pipe

RENAULT V10 RS1 ENGINE

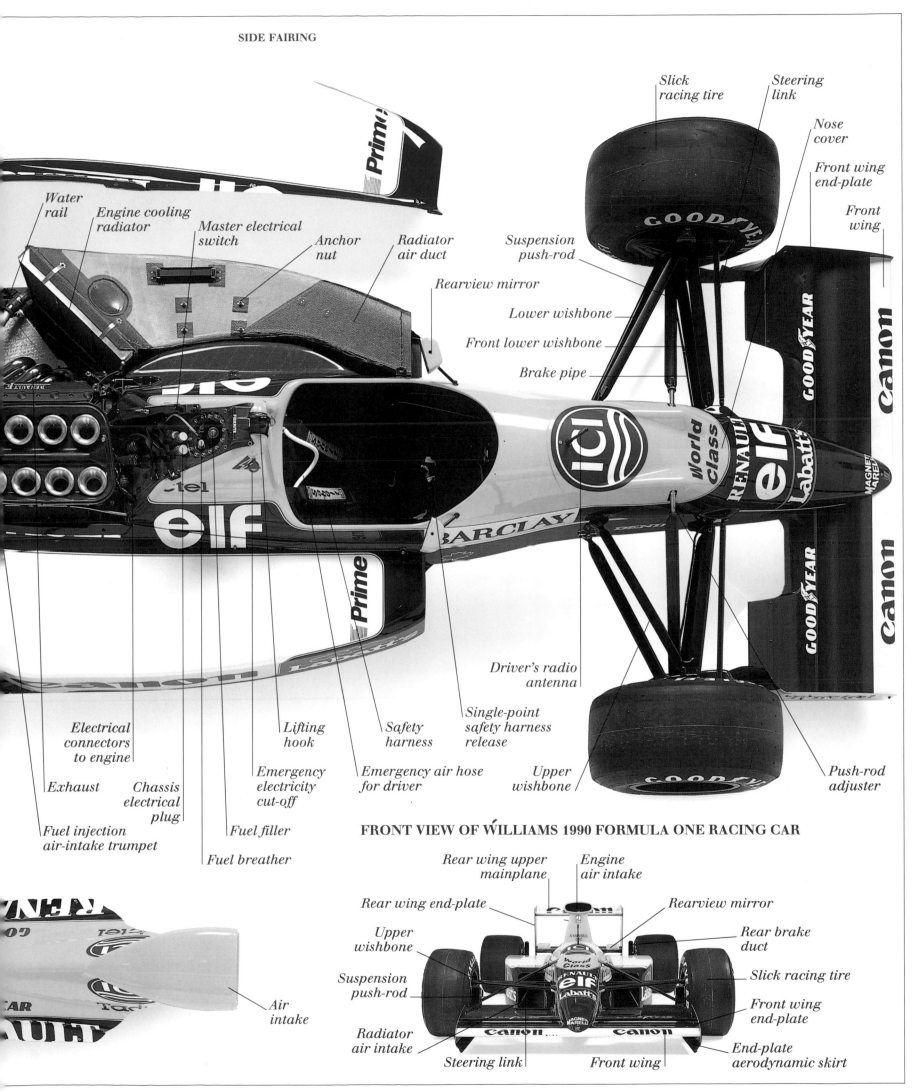

Water rail

Engine cooling radiator

Master electrical switch

Anchor nut

Radiator air duct

Slick racing tire

Steering link

Nose cover

Front wing end-plate

Front wing

Suspension push-rod

Rearview mirror

Lower wishbone

Front lower wishbone

Brake pipe

Electrical connectors to engine

Lifting hook

Safety harness

Single-point safety harness release

Driver's radio antenna

Exhaust

Chassis electrical plug

Emergency electricity cut-off

Emergency air hose for driver

Upper wishbone

Push-rod adjuster

Fuel injection air-intake trumpet

Fuel filler

Fuel breather

FRONT VIEW OF WILLIAMS 1990 FORMULA ONE RACING CAR

Rear wing upper mainplane

Engine air intake

Rear wing end-plate

Rearview mirror

Upper wishbone

Rear brake duct

Suspension push-rod

Slick racing tire

Air intake

Radiator air intake

Front wing end-plate

Steering link

Front wing

End-plate aerodynamic skirt

Index

60

Acknowledgments

Dorling Kindersley would like to thank the following:
Signore Amadelli, Museo dell' Automobile Carlo Biscaretti di Ruffia, for the Bordino Steam Carriage; Paul Bolton, Mazda MCL Group, for the Mazda RX-7 and the Wankel engine; Duncan Bradford of Reg Mills Wire Wheels, for the hub and wire racing wheel; John and Leslie Brewster, Autocavan, for Beetle spares; David Burgess-Wise, for the de Dion Bouton and Pilain clutch; Trevor Cass, Garrett Turbo Service, for the turbocharger; John Corbett, The Patrick Collection, for the Jaguar V12 engine; Gary Crumpler, Williams Grand Prix Engineering Ltd, for the Grand Prix car and engine; Mollie Easterbrooke and Duncan Gough, Overland Ltd, for the Pinzgauer Turbo D; Arthur Fairley, Vauxhall Motor Company, for the digitized instrument panel; Paul Foulkes-Halbard, Filching Manor Motor Museum, for the 70HP Mercedes and the Oldsmobile; Frank Gilbert, I. Wilkinson and Son Ltd, for the Rolls-Royce Silver Ghost "D" front limousine, the 1913 and 1924 Rolls-Royce Silver Ghost Tourers, the Alvis TL 12/60, and the Lanchester chassis; Paolo Gratton, Gratton Museum, for the Ford Model T; Colvin Gunn, of Gunn & Son, for the supercharger; Judy Hogg of Ecurie Bertelli, for the Aston Martin; Milton Holman, Dream Cars, for the Cadillac; Ian Matthews, IMAT

Electronics, for assistance; Eric Neal, Jaguar Cars Ltd, for the Jaguar engines, fascia, sectioned seat, and running gear, and for general assistance; Paul Niblett, Keith Davidson, Mark Reumel, and David Woolf, Michelin Tyre plc, for tyres and materials; Doug Nye, for assistance; Kevin O'Keefe, O'Keefe Cars, for the electric seat; Seat UK, for the Seat Ibiza; Roger Smith, for the Leyat; Jim Stirling, Ironbridge Gorge Museum, for the wooden wheel; Jon Taylor, for the Beetle; Doug Thompson, for the sprung seat; and Martyn Watkins, Ford Motor Company Ltd. In particular, for invaluable assistance and the supply of many items for photography: The National Motor Museum, Beaulieu; Alf Newell, Renault UK Ltd; David Suter, Cheltenham Cutaway Exhibits Ltd; and Francesca Riccini, Science Museum.

Additional photography:
Michelangelo Gratton of Vision, Peter Chadwick, Dave King, Nick Parfitt.

Additional editorial assistance:
Roger Tritton, Fiona Courtney-Thompson, Deirdre Clark.

Santa Fe Technical High School
2201 West Zia Road
Santa Fe, NM 87501
(505) 989-5524